CALENDAR OF LOVE

CALENDAR OF LOVE

BRIEF DAILY DEVOTIONAL READINGS THAT SHOW THE
DEVELOPMENT OF THE PRINCIPLE OF RIGHTEOUSNESS WITH
THE TRINITY OF LOVE WHICH IS THE LOVE OF GOD, RESPECT
FOR THE SELF AND LOVE TOWARD ALL PEOPLE

By

S. BURMAN LONG, D.D.

THE CHRISTOPHER PUBLISHING HOUSE
BOSTON, U.S.A.

This book is affectionately dedicated
to my wife, MARGARET HOCH LONG,
and our daughters
MARGARET LONG ARNOLD
And
CATHERINE LONG GLENDENING

PREFACE

Since doing advanced study with Dr. Ismar J. Peritz, Chairman of the Department of Bible at Syracuse University, my father has diligently continued to research the primitive notion of the wrath of God in contrast to the concept of God as a forgiving, helpful Father. My sister and I are pleased that he is sharing some of his findings in this Calendar of Love. You cannot help but be impressed by the depth of God's struggle to aid His people. A daily reading will nurture both spiritual and physical vigor and bring new understanding of your relationship with others and with God.

MARGARET LONG ARNOLD
(Mrs. Dexter Otis Arnold)
Honorary President
General Federation of Womens Clubs

Perhaps, in this ecumenical age, we need to think of God as active, righteous, love and personal rather than as revengeful and "dead." The Bible reveals as much. For a long time my father has pursued this thought with care and enthusiasm. In the *Calendar of Love* he shares the insights he has gleaned—a daily reminder of the efforts of God to reveal Himself as Righteousness and Love. It should provide comfort and stimulation for daily living and the sharing of human and Divine concerns.

CATHERINE LONG GLENDENING
(Mrs. John W. Glendening, Jr.)

FOREWORD

This book traces by *Titles, Texts, Daily Readings* and *Meditations* the idea that man should not be his own avenger. Experiences through time eventually led to the idea that vengeance was thought to belong to God as Sovereign. Primitive behavior patterns gradually grew into principles with RIGHTEOUSNESS as the goal and LOVE the method of living.

In the efforts to replace the vengeance of man, came laws, precepts and commandments to restrain the vicious, cruel, vengeful and unsocial elements of behavior. From these and with these were covenants and principles of conduct that were based on the RIGHTEOUSNESS and LOVE of God expressed and exemplified through the mind, heart, soul and strength of the individual and through the individual to the nation. This supreme characteristic of God as LOVE is supported by the commandment "you shall love your neighbor as yourself."

The understanding of the SELF is involved in the study as it is made clear that the GREAT COMMANDMENTS (Matthew 22:40) and the GOLDEN RULE (Matthew 7:12) each and together summarize the LAW AND THE PROPHETS.

As the individual reads each day's message with the Bible as the sourcebook, he will gradually and convincingly arrive at the basic understanding that GOD is SPIRIT, an active LOVING SPIRIT at work in individuals and nations to effect a will to live RIGHTEOUSLY with faith, hope and love.

S. Burman Long, D.D.
87 Monadnock Road
Worcester, Massachusetts

ACKNOWLEDGEMENTS

My thanks go to the many who have helped and encouraged me in this work—Drs. Ismar J. Peritz, George A. Wilson, Herbert Shenton, my teachers at Syracuse University. Walter A. Perry, South Weymouth, Mass., Mrs. Arthur W. Eldred, Worcester, Mass., Mr. and Mrs. Lawrence F. Hamilton, Auburn, Mass.

The Bible quotations, unless noted, are used by permission of Thomas Nelson and Sons from the Revised Standard Version. It should be used as a constant sourcebook.

Calendar of Love is intended to be read daily by individuals. These individuals should then meet with ten or twelve others on a weekly, bi-weekly or monthly basis to witness, analyze, discuss, criticize or express their own reactions and thoughts about their reading.

Calendar of Love

New Year's Day—January 1

LOVE IS FULFILLMENT

"Therefore love is the fulfilling of the law." (Romans 13:10b)

We begin the New Year with this premise that the author of the book of Romans states as a fact. What law does love fulfill? Is it the law of God when we think in terms of religion; a social law in terms of social science? To understand love is to know an orderly universe of persons. Love, in our human understanding, functions as gravity does in the physical world. Both are manifestations of God at work. One cannot ignore the power of love any more than he can that of gravity. To understand and to cooperate with the forces of love and gravity is to have a safe and orderly universe in which to live.

Meditation: Our heavenly Father, we accept the premise that You are Love, a real Loving Spirit. Speak to us by Your Spirit throughout the year. *Amen.*

January 2

LOVE WORKETH NO ILL

"Love does no wrong to a neighbor." (Romans 13:10a)

Yesterday we thought about LOVE as a principle of operation. Today we will give attention to the method of love's operation. Love in action fulfills the moral law. It comes to us from God and reaches to our neighbors. There is no limit or boundary to personal neighborliness. Love, like gravity, is

13

an operative force whether we cooperate with it or not. When a neighbor accepts the kindness of a neighbor both may be benefitted. Although a neighbor may not accept or return the kindness, yet the doer of the kindness is edified. A person may reject the love and kindness of another but he cannot destroy love and kindness. Love is a positive force.

Meditation: The eternity of love is in the heart of God and man, and is beyond both time and space. May God's Love support me at all times and places! Your hands, O God, are stronger than human hands. Therefore, I am not afraid to face this day and every day. *Amen.*

January 3

GOD'S GOODNESS IS APPROVED

"In the beginning God." (Genesis 1:1a)

The tradition and philosophy of Christianity, Judaism and Islam is that the universe began with God. We begin our study with God. Just when people began to think of God as Spirit that brought order out of chaos we do not know. We do not need to know. It is enough to know that the passing of eras of time and many experiences led to the thought that God was a moving Spirit that brought order. The author of these introductory verses in Genesis, like Jesus, assumed that God is an active Spirit at work and that we have an active physical as well as an active moral order.

Meditation: Our Father, keep us thinking that life is worthwhile. May we believe that it is better to be than not to be. We thank You for the gift of life. *Amen.*

January 4

LIGHT OF THE WORLD

"God said . . . 'Let there be light', and there was light." (Genesis 1:3)

Meditation: "Lord of all being, throned afar, Thy glory flames from sun and star. Center and soul of every sphere, yet to each loving heart how near!" Oliver Wendell Holmes, from Hymn "Lord of All Being Throned Afar"

January 8
WHAT IS MAN!

"God said, '. . . the man has become like one of us, knowing good and evil.' " (Genesis 3:22)

It is assumed here that God knows good and evil. Both good and evil are regarded as real. Man being something like God also knows both good and evil. Both good and evil exist and as human beings we can choose one or the other or both. If the good is chosen one never comes to a dead end. If the evil is chosen there is moral death. Persons made decisions then. They can make decisions now. We have moral insight. We are free to choose good or evil. We are free persons.

Meditation: Thanks, O God, for personality. Help each one of us to choose the good instead of the evil this day and every day. Chastise me when I may do evil so that I may review my decisions and acts and be induced henceforth to do the good. *Amen.*

January 9
MY BROTHER'S KEEPER

"Am I my brother's keeper?" (Genesis 4:9c)

The answer is, yes. To choose to be unconcerned about wrong that is done to another is a poor choice. If we care we will share. If we help we may be helped. Cain asked the question too late. Abel was already dead. Mankind is bound together by God's creative Spirit. The fact that Cain asked the question is evidence that his conscience plagued him. The distortion of good is evil. Through God's creative plan there is moral insight that plagues the guilty person when wrong is done and praises when good is done. That Cain became angry evidences guilt. Let us always be concerned about our brother and obey the inner conscience that may be the highest arbiter.

Meditation: Help me to be thoughtful and helpful to others. It may be others will be brotherly to me. In You, O God, I put my trust. May the goodness that You give to me be freely given to others! *Amen.*

January 10
GOD CARES FOR WHAT HE HAS CREATED

"If any one slays Cain, vengeance shall be taken on him sevenfold." (Genesis 4:15b)

Most scholars think that Cain was a tribe. Whether he was an individual or a tribe the importance of being concerned about the welfare of a brother had not yet been learned. In what appears to have been an argument Cain had killed his brother Abel. The question was whether man should make retribution for the killing of the only man or tribe that was left within God's creatorship. Should a beast or person or persons from another possible tribe kill Cain as a retributive act? God said, "No." He said that Cain should be protected and decreed that a sevenfold punishment would be given to any person or tribe that would kill Cain. It seems as if the killing of man for retribution's sake is not in God's plan. God wanted to preserve the life of Cain although he had done wrong. Does this evidence of God's protection to an offender have meaning for us?

Meditation: Help us our Father to remember that this is Your universe and that You will care for what You have created. May we never assume that we are justified to destroy man whom You have created! *Amen.*

January 11
THE VENGEANCE OF LAMECH

"If Cain is avenged sevenfold, truly Lamech seventy-seven-fold." (Genesis 4:24)

In this portion of an ancient poem Lamech appears to be defending his right to be vengeful and cruel by telling two of his wives that vengeance evidenced his great strength and was therefore justified. He claimed the right of unlimited vengeance. He was wrong. He is typical of the conduct of primitive social practice. Centuries later Jesus, in his conversation with Peter, reversed the primitive system of Lamech after being asked by Simon Peter, "how often shall my brother sin against me, and I forgive him? As many as seven times?" (Matthew 18:21b) He replied, "I do not say to you seven times, but seventy times seven." (Matthew 18:22b) This suggests unlimited forgiveness against the primitive notion of unlimited revenge. We now have the basis of our study which is to search and to find the steps that have led to a change of the practice of unlimited forgiveness instead of the primitive one of unlimited revenge as a basis of social action. Although Cain had done wrong he was still a child of God's creation.

Meditation: May we never as individuals revert to the primitive assumption that we are justified in being revengeful and cruel toward others. May the society in which we live regard itself as a redemptive power. *Amen.*

January 12
MAN LEARNS TO WALK WITH GOD

"Enoch walked with God." (Genesis 5:24a)

Some time ago in ancient history men learned that if mankind would continue to exercise revenge the end would be extinction. It was also learned that when men like Enoch walked with God and worked in the Spirit of God they lived longer. Because Enoch seems to have done the will of God he came to be with God. Do we have an intimation of immortality and the resurrection here? The man who chooses good never dies!

Meditation: May each of us walk with You now and hereafter! Make each of us sensitive and responsive to the leading of Your Spirit. May inner peace prevail. Make peace communicable through each of us. *Amen.*

January 13

NOAH IS FAVORED

"But Noah found favor in the eyes of the Lord." (Genesis 6:8)

Lamech had assumed a power as if he were a god. Noah regarded favorably the power and judgment of God. He built the ark according to God's direction for his own welfare and the welfare of others. The wicked were those who would not obey the advice of Noah and enter the ark, whereas the righteous obeyed God and Noah and entered the ark. (Genesis 7:1c) The flood incident evidenced the overthrow of the wicked and the saving values of those who were righteous and obedient. We learn as we read these verses that God is in control.

Meditation: Help us to learn for ourselves that each life has times of testing. May we have learned as truth that wickedness destroys the evil doer but that righteousness with obedience has saving values! *Amen.*

January 14

NOAH OPENED THE WINDOW

"Noah opened the window of the ark which he had made." (Genesis 8:6b)

The ark was a ship of safety. Noah, however, was not content to remain indefinitely in the ark. Freedom with God's guidance was in his spirit. His soul longed to be free and when the rain abated he opened the window. He used the actions of the dove to guide him. Do you think the survival of the dove and Noah's will to be guided had anything to teach concerning the securing and maintaining of life? Is there any significance in the dove of Noah with the dove-like Spirit that came upon Jesus at the time of His baptism? (Matthew 3:16)

Meditation: May we, like Noah, build the ark of Spiritual faith to keep us from evil. May we keep the windows of the mind open for the Holy Spirit's entrance. Let us obey God, build solidly to endure and withstand every evil wind that blows. *Amen.*

January 15
THE RAINBOW A SIGN OF THE COVENANT

"I establish my covenant with you." (Genesis 9:11a)
"I set my bow in the cloud, and it shall be a sign of the covenant." (Genesis 9:13)

God does not like destruction. He wants mankind to do right and to live, but the universe is created so that wickedness and destruction travel together, and righteousness and continued life go on together. We have learned in our study of Cain that wickedness, guilt and death travel together but here we learn that righteousness, obedience and life continue together. The rainbow was regarded as a reminder of the saving covenant that God had made with mankind. God had continued to communicate with man. The rainbow is a reminder of God's saving grace. We are right in thinking of a rainbow as beautiful to the sight and a reminder of the saving value of obedience to God.

Meditation: Help me to keep the promises I have made to You and those that I have made to myself. May the recurring rainbow remind me of Your care and concern for all people.

You will keep the covenant. Help me to keep my part of it! *Amen.*

January 16

GOD BLESSED NOAH

"God blessed Noah." (Genesis 9:1a)

God is here represented as blessing Noah, who obeyed God's communications and was worthy of being favored. It is apparent that Noah was aware of the forces of nature as active and made himself and others with him secure within the ark. Noah accepted the communications as coming from God. His foresight with faith and manual preparation saved the human race from extinction. Life continued, the flood abated and Noah became the progenitor of persons who may have become leaders of tribes. It is clear that Noah's future conduct was not always exemplary. He had to experiment and to learn the hard way. The excessive use of the fruit of the vineyard was not pleasing to God or to Noah's sons. It created division within the family. History has regarded Noah's conduct as sinful but God in His mercy allowed survival to continue. The lack of control on the part of Noah was not approved by God or man.

Meditation: Help me, O God, to hear Your words and to obey them! Help us to love what You love and do what You would have us do! *Amen.*

January 17

ABRAHAM: A MAN OF THE COVENANT

"And they went forth together from Ur of the Chaldeans to go into the land of Canaan." (Genesis 11:31c)

This is the best place to begin a study of the teachings of the Bible. Abram, later named Abraham, was a pioneer. He was historically regarded as the father of the Hebrew people who migrated from Ur of the Chaldeans to Canaan. It is apparent that his idea about God and worship differed from that of the Chaldeans and he ventured forth with faith. Later, when his pioneer efforts were appraised, it was recognized that he had been led by God and had a definite mission. A study of the worship of the primitive Chaldeans will help us to appreciate the genius and pioneering spirit and mind of Abraham.

Meditation: Help us to follow the leadership of God! Make me a pioneer of truth! Lead us to the mountain of noble thinking and correct judgment! May faith in Your guiding be increased as we read about further experiences of Abraham! *Amen.*

January 18
ABRAHAM WORSHIPS GOD IN CANAAN

"He built an altar to the Lord and called on the name of the Lord." (Genesis 12:8c)

Many of the insights in the earlier chapters of Genesis stem from concepts about God that Abraham had. The erection of a simple altar on a hill which was called Bethel (house of the Lord) became the seed of the thought that any place or condition where one worships God is a "house of God." Abraham was aware of a Supreme Being, but about His name he was uncertain. He knew that it was a name that meant blessing, favor, guidance and righteousness. To him God was approachable and intimate. He knew that conduct was involved in the worship of God. He knew the Spirit of God even if he did not know His name. He accepted the leadership of a force greater than himself.

Meditation: Help us to cooperate with others in making worship primary in everyday living. May we accept the notion that the idea of the righteousness of God is inherent and that God delights in righteousness. *Amen.*

January 19

A FORMULA FOR PEACE

"If you take the left hand, then I will go to the right; or if you take the right hand, then I will go to the left." (Genesis 13:9)

The increase of Abraham's flocks and possessions and those of his nephew, Lot, created a problem in the new land to which they had come. A threatened strife of the herdsmen of the two men was averted when the two men with their flocks and possessions were willing to separate for the sake of peace. Each would remain free. The magnanimity of Abraham is shown by his willingness to accept second choice. Is the conduct on the part of these two men a root idea to have peace and freedom? Did Abraham or Lot make the better choice? Upon what does success depend?

Meditation: Our Father in Heaven, we rejoice because Abraham trusted in Your guidance and was not afraid. His willingness to take the second choice may be an example for all of us. May we realize that second choice with God is better than first choice without God! *Amen.*

January 20

THE CHOICE OF LOT

"So Lot chose for himself all the Jordan valley, and Lot journeyed east." (Genesis 13:11a)

We must remember that the land of Canaan was inhabited. The Jordan plain was fertile and included the cities of Sodom and Gomorrah. Abraham's area was the least fertile of Mamre in Hebron and it was here that he built an altar to worship God. For the sake of peace Abraham and Lot separated but it did not separate Abraham from his God. Is separation a value or disvalue? In reading about the future of these two men or tribes do you think it was the areas of land or the characters of the two leaders that determined the success of the one and the failure of the other? How much influence has environment?

Meditation: We are grateful for the examples of persons like Abraham who are willing to cooperate with God for the sake of peace and freedom. May my intimacy with God and my magnanimity be as conclusive and genuine as was that of Abraham! *Amen.*

January 21

THE SHIELD OF ABRAHAM

"The word of the Lord came to Abram . . . 'Fear not, I am your shield.' " (Genesis 15:1)

The constant trouble with herdsmen and the realization that he had no heir troubled Abraham. The satisfaction that God was his shield encouraged him as he worshipped. A reading of this fifteenth chapter shows how the covenant and the notion of the intimacy of God grew out of the primitive method of worship. It was through the worship of God that Abraham received a response from God that He was his shield. The devotion and sacrificial spirit of Abraham was accepted by God. Does the thought of God being a shield mean that God would protect Abraham and his descendants regardless of conduct?

Meditation: Will You be a shield to us just as You shielded and led Abraham? May each of us keep any covenant that we may have made with You. May we go forward in peace knowing that Your Spirit is with us! *Amen.*

January 22

ABRAHAM AND GOD MAKE A COVENANT

"The Lord made a covenant with Abram." (Genesis 15:18a)

Abraham prepared a sacrificial meal for himself and God by placing the sacrificial animals in parallel rows. God responded to his worship by giving light, heat and smoke that appeared as a flaming torch. This, to Abraham, signified the presence and response of God in that it gave him assurance, protection and possession. The torch with light and heat assured the sealing of the covenant. Abraham was convinced that God was with him. Do you think there is any connection between the flaming torch that Abraham saw and the Holy Spirit when it descended upon Jesus? (Matthew 3:16)

Meditation: We thank you God that we belong to a covenant people. We believe that God will help and protect us when and if we live right. We pray for daily strength. May we be faithful in keeping our part of the covenant. May our worship help us and please You! *Amen.*

January 23

EXILE IS EMBARRASSING

"Thou art a God of seeing." (Genesis 16:13b)

We now move from the tribal to the family way of living. Abraham wanted an heir. Sarah his wife was childless. Hagar, the handmaid, conceived and became the mother of Ishmael. Later Sarah became the mother of Isaac. Sarah, the legitimate wife, became jealous and Hagar, the concubine, and Ishmael were exiled. In the wilderness exile she found a spring of water. Here an angel appeared and urged her to return and submit to Sarah as a slave. She took second place. The descendants of Ishmael were called Ishmaelites and the descendants of Sarah became known as Israelites. They thought of themselves as the legitimate descendants of Abraham and his wife Sarah while the Ishmaelites, lated called Edomites, were descendants of the illegitimate slave woman. They were regarded as being of lower caste. The Israelites regarded themselves as the purer and legitimate descendants of Sarah and Abraham.

Meditation: May we always find a well of prayer! Although some persons may be unjust, we know that You are just. As

God answered the prayer of Hagar and she and the life of the child were saved, so may we seek Your help in times of stress. *Amen.*

January 24
ABRAHAM HAS A LEGITIMATE HEIR
"I will establish my covenant with Isaac." (Genesis 17:21a)

The covenant that God and Abraham made was continued through Isaac. Isaac as the legitimate heir continued the ancestry of the people of Israel, whereas Ishmael was regarded as the illegitimate heir. His descendants were called Ishmaelites and by others, and at a later time, Edomites. The word Isaac means laughter. Does this suggest that the religion of the Israelites suggests *joy* or only that Abraham and Sarah were happy to have a son and heir?

Meditation: Help us to remember that we are a covenant people. May I not fail to keep my part of the covenant, for history has taught that God does not fail to keep His part. May I always do Your will! *Amen.*

January 25
HOSPITALITY IS REWARDED
"Let a little water be brought, and wash your feet and rest . . . while I fetch a morsel of bread, that you may refresh yourselves." (Genesis 18:4a-5a)

This is a case of entertaining angels unaware. The three strangers that were welcomed by Abraham proved to be messengers of God. They announced that Sarah and Abraham would have an heir. The birth of Isaac was thought by some to be impossible because of the age of Sarah but it shows that there is nothing impossible with God. The prayer of Abraham was answered. Is the hospitality of Abraham contributory to the principle that the Christian religion is often expressed through kindness, forgiveness and hospitality?

Meditation: Help us always to be alert to Your presence. May we always remember that You are working through us and that we should never lose faith in You or in ourselves. *Amen.*

January 26
ABRAHAM INTERVENES FOR THE RIGHTEOUS

"For the sake of ten I will not destroy it." (Genesis 18:32d)

Lot's choice of the Jordan valley, where Sodom and Gomorrah were located, brought him and the members of his family or tribe among people who did not worship the God of Abraham. On account of their wickedness they were destroying themselves. Ultimate annihilation was impending. Abraham had compassion on them and tried to save them. Even ten righteous persons could save the cities but they could not be found. Because of Abraham's intervention a few righteous were saved. It is the nature of God to save the righteous. Does the word Abraham possibly mean "father of compassion?" Abraham is generally accepted to mean "father of a multitude" but the word "Ab" means "father" and the Hebrew word "racham" means compassion.

Meditation: We rejoice because of the compassion of Abraham. Like Abraham help us to use our intelligence and influence to help others to escape the effects of wickedness. Help us to save the wicked by Your Righteousness! *Amen.*

January 27

LOT SHARES

"They . . . entered his house; and he made them a feast." (Genesis 19:3b)

Lot was hospitable to persons whom he afterwards learned were messengers of God. This welcome aroused suspicions among the citizens of Sodom. They were so depraved that they could not appreciate kindness. As a result of their suspicions the conduct of the people of Sodom toward Lot and his family does not make good reading for Christians. It shows the nature of the conduct of people who have no concept or belief in a righteous God. The citizens of the two cities would not listen to reason. Can we conclude that wicked people who do not know a God of Love and Compassion may never reason rightly? When the premises are wrong the conclusions are wrong. The people of Sodom and Gomorrah were so ignorant and wicked that they would not appreciate kindness.

Meditation: We are thankful for the preservation of the record that shows the courage of Lot in a difficult situation. As he fled the wicked cities so may we flee wickedness. May we never choose to remain where there is wickedness! *Amen.*

January 28
ABRAHAM IS TREATED WITH KINDNESS

"Abimelech said, 'Behold my land is before you; dwell where it pleases you.'" (Genesis 20:15)

Abraham seems to have been disgusted on account of the wickedness of the people in the area and moved farther south into the territory of Abimelech, king of Gerar. The hospitality of Abimelech was reciprocated by Abraham to the advantage of both. Abimelech and Abraham both had a sense of the value of good human relations. Can we conclude that wrongdoing promotes wrongdoing and right relations encourage congenial fellowship?

Meditation: May we remember that there may be a spirit of righteousness in every person. Sin may smother it, evil practices harden it, suspicions deaden it, perverted judgments ignore it, but it is still there. Help each of us to keep alive the spiritual power we call conscience! *Amen.*

January 29

THE MORALS ARE WEAK

"There is no fear of God at all in this place." (Genesis 20:11b)

The family life in this period was insecure and unstable. It is probable that the lack of ethical patterns in the areas of Sodom and Gomorrah had made Abraham suspicious of the morals in Gerar and Egypt. In both places the zeal for self preservation caused Abraham to resort to deception. In both cases the morals of the leaders were higher than Abraham had supposed. Neither the Pharaoh of Egypt nor Abimelech approved of his deception. He was apparently unaware of inherent family rightness. Because of his own misconduct and subsequent guilt Abraham may have received an added incentive to worship and to call upon the Everlasting God. We must remember that we are dealing and reading about primitive people as we read chapters 12, 20, 26, etc. in Genesis.

Meditation: Let us obey God even when we are frustrated. May we remember that there is always a well of spiritual water available although we may be in the wilderness of pagan associates! *Amen.*

January 30

ABRAHAM HEARS GOD

"God will provide himself the lamb for a burnt offering my son." (Genesis 22:8)

It is clear that Abraham lived among neighboring tribes that felt their gods needed to be appeased by sacrifice. Abraham felt that his God was as efficient, powerful and deserving as the gods of his neighbor tribes and he was willing to offer as great a sacrifice. They sacrificed their firstborn and Abraham was willing to do as much. However, his conscience was not clear and he asked for guidance. The answer came. God intervened and provided an animal sacrifice. It may have dawned upon him that his God did not want appeasement, but devotion and service. It is possible that the conscience of Abraham, his love for Isaac and his intimacy with God gave him a higher insight into God's demands, loyalty and methods of worship.

Meditation: O God it is Your concern to preserve and to continue life rather than to take it. May we help You to preserve life on earth through the medium of peace! *Amen.*

January 31

HITTITE PHILOSOPHY

"I give you the field, and I give you the cave that is in it." (Genesis 23:11)

When Sarah died, Ephron, the Hittite, having observed the generosity of Abraham, offered him the cave of Machepelah as a burial plot. This gift shows the cooperation of neighborliness with those who are neighborly. Ephron may have admired the God of Abraham because of the conduct of Abraham. Death also tends to make neighbors neighborly and generous. Sympathy and compassion beget hospitality and friendship.

Meditation: Help me to be gracious to those who dislike me as well as to those who like me. May the spirit of compassion prevail in me. Help each of us to be aware that we are not completely efficient within ourselves. Help me to be a good neighbor! *Amen.*

February 1

ABRAHAM LOOKS TOWARD THE FUTURE

"Blessed be the Lord, the God of my master Abraham, who has not forsaken his steadfast love and his faithfulness toward my master." (Genesis 24:27)

Abraham did not want his son Isaac to marry one of the natives. He sent his trusted servant with Isaac to Mesopotamia where Nahor, Abraham's brother, lived to seek a wife for Isaac. In the journey the caravan stopped at an oasis. It was here that Rebekah, daughter of Nahor, had come to draw water. She was generous and shared the water, and the servant in oriental fashion revealed his mission. Rebekah was interested and although they belonged to kindred tribes she consented to become the wife of Isaac. Does this have any relation to our problem of segregation?

Meditation: The effort of Abraham to keep pagan ways and customs out of his family connections was rewarded with a blessing. May our family life be kept pure and worshipful so that we may be worthy of Your blessing and continued guidance! *Amen.*

February 2

ISAAC LOVES REBEKAH

"Rebekah . . . became his wife; and he loved her. So Isaac was comforted after his mother's death." (Genesis 24:67b)

Rebekah proved to be a modest, faithful wife. The guidance of God and their willingness to be guided had brought them together. The Hebrew word AHAB is translated love and means deep personal love that revers and respects the object of this love. If love is deep in the sense of sincerity it is also high in the sense of sharing. Love is subjective but there must be an object such as God, person or persons to be loved. The approval of the union by Abraham and the servants is commendable. Many oriental customs are described in this twenty-fourth chapter. Do you agree that in our study the family is becoming a unit for happiness?

Meditation: Your Love is the highest Love. If we love You it is only natural that we should love people. May the high Love of God as we know it at work among the Hebrew people, Jesus and His disciples be a factor in the faith of all of us! *Amen.*

February 3

FALSE PARENTAL AMBITION MAY DIVIDE

"Isaac loved Esau . . . but Rebekah loved Jacob." (Genesis 25:28)

Isaac and Rebekah were parents of the twins, Esau and Jacob. Esau was born first and had the oriental right of primogeniture. Jacob, however, had a personal quality that appealed to Rebekah. She favored Jacob, the younger. According to the oriental pattern Esau should have received the birthright and blessing of the father. This incident shows the strength of parental love. Should parents show favoritism? Can favoritism be avoided?

Meditation: Help us to love as You love. You breathed something of Yourself into us. We should let this "breath of God" guide us. As parents help us to live and to act so that there shall arise in our children no question about the power of genuine love! *Amen.*

February 4

PEACE PREVAILS

"We have found water." (Genesis 26:32c)

When Isaac and the members of his tribe moved into the area of Gerar they faced the problem of water. Isaac persisted in digging until they found water which they shared with the people of Gerar. This fellowship led to further revelations of God that assured them that the covenant with Abraham was also a covenant with the descendants of Abraham. The generosity of the Israelites in sharing the well, Rehobeth, with the people of Gerar was appreciated and their friendship was augmented. Is it true that the sharing of anything good like water brings one closer to those with whom it is shared? Why is it advantageous to eat and to commune together?

Meditation: May the present peace among nations inspire us to share our surplus. May we realize that generosity and sharing have their source in creative loving! *Amen.*

February 5
ISAAC BLESSES HIS SONS

"Bless me, even me also, O my father." (Genesis 27:34c)

This is a cry of bitterness and disappointment. In keeping with an ancient custom the birthright and blessing should have been given to the older son, Esau. But Rebekah, being partial toward Jacob, contrived that the blind father, Isaac, bestow the birthright and first blessing upon Jacob. This deception created an estrangement. Esau, according to custom, was justified in being angry. The result of this deception was the breaking up of the home and the exiling of Jacob. Deception, however cleverly planned, always creates friction and sometimes it leads to estrangement.

Meditation: Keep my home intact. May my deepest love and blessing go to all the members of my family. May parental love teach and exemplify the Love of God! May parental and childlike love prevail in my home! *Amen.*

February 6
JACOB IS NOT FORSAKEN

"Surely the Lord is in this place." (Genesis 28:16b)
"This is the gate of heaven." (Genesis 28:17)

Isaac, like Abraham, did not want his son to marry a native girl. In his blessing he urged Jacob to go to Paddan-aram where the kindred of his mother Rebekah lived. Because of his deception he actually had to flee to save his own life. The journey was far and unplanned. He was an exile. With a deep feeling of despair and guilt he slept under the skies, in the open. During the night he dreamed of a ladder that reached to heaven with angels ascending and descending upon it. This dream convinced him that God had not forsaken him. This sense of God being with him although he was guilty of deception gave him courage to continue the journey and mission.

Meditation: Help us to sense that Heaven is around us, that it is more a condition than a place. May the knowledge that God is present help us to keep our faith and integrity! *Amen.*

February 7

JACOB MAKES A VOW

"If God will be with me . . . so that I come again to my father's house in peace, then the Lord shall be my God." (Genesis 28:20-21)

The awareness of God's presence eased the fear and guilt of Jacob. The God of Abraham had continued to be his God. He made a vow. He accepted the covenant relationship. He found his kinfolk and married both Leah and Rachel, daughters of Laban, and returned after many years to his homeland. He found Esau to be gracious and forgiving when he returned. The hard years of toil and service with Laban kept him close to God. However, the history of Israel might have been different if Jacob had not deceived his father. Can we say that filial deception is never good?

Meditation: Help us to be honest with all people. May we be honorable and upright with You today and every day. May every temptation to deceive be smothered with nobler thoughts and acts! *Amen.*

February 8

THE POWER OF LOVE

"Jacob served seven years for Rachel, and they seemed to him but a few days because of the love he had for her." (Genesis 29:20)

A careful reading indicates that Jacob actually served fourteen years for Rachel. The span of years seemed brief because of his love. Love proves to be a satisfying and unifying force. It is sacrificial in that Jacob served Laban fourteen years. Love is personal and cannot be divided. To attempt to divide love is to create emotional and intellectual frustration. Love is a perfect science. "Perfect love casts out fear." Love defines the real Jacob in contrast to the guilt-confused Jacob. Love kept Jacob purposeful and loyal to his vow. Do you think Jacob was really happy during the years of exile while he was serving Laban?

Meditation: Help me to love as the angels love. Keep me true to those who love me. May those I love be worthy and may I be worthy of those who love me! *Amen.*

February 9
JACOB AND LABAN MAKE A COVENANT AT MIZPAH

"The Lord watch between you and me, when we are absent one from the other." (Genesis 31:49c)

When Jacob and Laban separated, Jacob took his wives, children and property with him. A concern arose because Rachel had taken the household gods with her, although there seemed to be a superstition that anyone taking these gods should not live. Yet Laban was forgiving and before he left to return to his home they ate together and made a covenant and sealed it with the above words. They built an altar and set up stones as a witness. Does this incident show that when parental and filial love exist forgiveness becomes a by-product?

Meditation: Thank you God because we are again reminded that forgiveness and concern for the welfare of others brings peace and reconciliation. May our trust in You rid us of malice, jealousy, covetousness and suspicion! May the above words be a benediction upon me and my family! *Amen.*

February 10
JACOB PRAYS FOR FORGIVENESS

"Deliver me, I pray thee, from the hand of my brother . . . for I fear him." (Genesis 32:11a)

Jacob finally returned to his homeland with his family and possessions after at least twenty years of exile. Because of his deceptions and guilt he was afraid of Esau. Would Esau continue the feud and kill him? The mental punishment was severe. The years of exile were as years in slavery. He came, however, to be thought of as the true Israelite because his father and mother were kindred. He was the legitimate heir and his own wives were of kindred stock. Esau on the other hand had married girls of Canaan. One of his wives was a Hittite. To the Jews today Jacob and his descendants constitute the pure Jewish genealogy.

Meditation: May we remember that if we do wrong we will be punished. The nature of the universe decrees this. Restore every divided home by Your power of forgiveness and love. May we be encouraged by Jacob's desire for forgiveness and Esau's willingness to forgive! *Amen.*

February 11
JACOB RECEIVES FURTHER ASSURANCE

"For I have seen God face to face, and yet my life is preserved." (Genesis 32:30b)

Before the guilty Jacob met Esau he was alone at the brook Jabbok. Here he wrestled with God. May it be that he wrestled with his own conscience? Could he show true repentance and friendliness to Esau? Would Esau forgive him? He decided to advance with caution by placing the children ahead like a flag of truce. Having a changed attitude in himself he prayed that Esau might also. His prayer was answered. Esau was not revengeful. God's concern for him was again confirmed.

Meditation: Let, O Lord, the example of these brothers inspire me and others to be forgiving and to live in peace. May the power of love supplant envy, jealousy, mistreatment and any desire of will in me to do harm! *Amen.*

February 12
THE BROTHERS MEET AMICABLY

"Esau ran to meet him, and embraced him . . . and kissed him." (Genesis 33:4)

What a subject for a painter! The primitive custom of unlimited revenge and even the idea of "like for like" had been broken down by the two brothers. The devotion to God in them was stronger than enmity or custom. Both brothers sensed the idea that God was their God and He had not forsaken them. Forgiveness prevailed and availed. Love proved stronger than physical force. Both men sought forgiveness and the blessing of God. The God of Abraham, Isaac and Jacob was still their God and peace was the fruitage. Were both men happier because of the reconciliation?

Meditation: May we also wrestle with the self within us and it may be that we also shall see the face of God. It may be that the person whom we fear as an enemy wants friendship. In any estrangement may a reconciliation be effected rather than to continue to live in fear and with guilt. Help me to live with myself! *Amen.*

February 13
GRACE HELPS IN SEEING GOD

"Truly to see your face is like seeing the face of God, with such favor have you received me." (Genesis 33:10c)

What a revelation! The graciousness of Esau was to Jacob like looking at the face of God. The spirit of compassion embodied in Abraham was demonstrated and the reconciliation prevailed. Brotherly love had worked what envy could not have done. This instance of filial reconciliation shows that a stream of love with forgiveness had begun to flow from the heart and will of God. The household of Isaac and Rebekah had gone but the Spirit of God prevailed in their sons.

Meditation: We thank you, O God, for the universal law of love. We know that love is a unifying force which makes for righteousness. May the United Nations personnel be guided by the power of love! May we always hold that reconciliation is better than war and strife! *Amen.*

February 14
THE NAME OF GOD

"And God said to him, 'I am God Almighty.'" (Genesis 35:11a)

It was difficult to apply a name to the Supreme Being of the patriarchs. Jacob named the place where he confronted God, Bethel, which means "house of God." Later Jacob himself was named Israel which means "prince of God." Our text uses the Hebrew word El Shaddai which is translated "God Almighty." It is apparent that these names grew out of exceptionable experiences. El Shaddai suggests a powerful God who cared for the welfare of the people of Israel. He was their supreme guiding power.

Meditation: O God, we approach You with reverence. Like the Israelites we have constant need of Your guiding Spirit. May the churches and altars where we worship be meaningful. May I never leave You or forsake You! *Amen.*

February 15
LOVE SHOULD BE KEPT IN CONTROL

"Israel loved Joseph . . . and his brethren saw that their father loved him more than all his brethren." (Genesis 37:3, 4 A.V.)

Joseph was one of twelve brothers and sons of Jacob. He

seems to have been ambitious, thoughtful, kind and highly religious. He may have been more amiable than the brothers and Jacob admired his qualities. The fact that Joseph was the older of the two sons of Rachel, his favorite wife, may have had some psychological influence in regarding him as a favorite son. Evidently the high love of Jacob for Joseph was genuine and could not be hidden. The brothers resented this favoritism. They showed their envy and jealousy in word and deed. Did the brothers err in being envious and unbrotherly? Would they have been edified if they had patterned their ways after those of Joseph?

Meditation: Let love be without dissimulation. May we never despise or envy the success and well-being of another. Let us have unfailing confidence in right. Let us remember that betraying another will harm the betrayer. Let us love a brother as we love You! *Amen.*

February 16

JOSEPH IS TAKEN TO EGYPT

"But the Lord was with Joseph and showed him steadfast love." (Genesis 39:21)

The description of the envious brothers of Joseph and their treatment of him does not make pleasant reading. It shows that the brothers were primitive in judgment and decorum. Even the dialogue among the brothers about what they should do with Joseph shows their inward confusion. The final decision to sell him to the caravan traders was about the worst they could do or think. On the other hand, whether Joseph was searching for his brothers in Dothan or a slave in Egypt he showed a good spirit, wisdom, discernment, self control and trust in God. He was willing to be guided by the compass of Righteousness. Do you think that the reading and telling about Joseph may have had any influence upon the future mission of Jesus? Do you think Jesus read or heard the history of Joseph when he was a boy in Nazareth?

Meditation: Our Father, we thank You for persons with character like Joseph. We are grateful that the record of his life and conduct has been preserved and made available for us. May we never be unbrotherly as were the brothers of Joseph! *Amen.*

February 17

JOSEPH IS PROVED

"Can we find such a man as this, in whom is the Spirit of God?" (Genesis 41:38)

The Pharaoh in Egypt was a difficult man with whom to deal. He knew not the God of Joseph. He did, however, perceive the wisdom of Joseph and attributed it to the presence of the Spirit of God. The future conduct of Joseph showed that the faith and trust that the Pharaoh had in him was well founded. Even the pagan Pharaoh could discern in him superior strength and capabilities. The Pharaoh was aware of the presence in Joseph of a power that had guiding force to one who trusted Him. Joseph withstood the severest tests but the wisdom and trust he had in God helped him to withstand temptation and to succeed.

Meditation: Help us realize that we can help others best by having command of the Self! *Amen.*

February 18

JOSEPH IS AFRAID TO DISOBEY GOD

"Joseph said . . . 'Do this and you will live, for I fear God.'" (Genesis 42:18)

It appears that righteousness had become almost a sixth sense with Joseph. He did right and obeyed God so long that it was almost instinctive to do right. He chose to suffer unjustly rather than to do evil. This supreme conduct was even

observed and noted by the pagan Pharaoh and finally by the
guilty brothers also. Their plight led Reuben to confess how
they saw the distress of the soul of Joseph when they put him
in the pit and sold him to the leader of the caravan. He explained that their situation in Egypt was a result of their unbrotherliness and that it seems to have been within the plan
of the universe or cosmos to punish wrongdoing. Unbrotherliness, it was clear, was wrong. The famine had accentuated
their sense of guilt. Wrongdoing creates guilt and the depri-
vation pointed it up. Because the brothers were in distress
and sought for a cause is good psychology.
Meditation: We ask, O God, for the high love of Yourself to
be in us. We know that evil will ultimately fail but that
righteousness will support us even in hazardous situations.
Keep my conscience clean and my mind pure! *Amen.*

February 19
JOSEPH IS SUPPORTED BY HIS FAITH
"May God Almighty grant you mercy before the man."
(Genesis 43:14)
     These are the words of Jacob to his sons when famine
had come. They had heard that there was food in Egypt and
Jacob had faith that God would help them and they would
find favor from the one in Egypt who controlled the food supply. The brothers went to Egypt and found favor with the
man in charge of the granaries whom they later learned was
their own brother, Joseph. The one whom they had wronged
had become their saviour. This revelation of God's care and
support of righteousness in a person was beyond their expectation. It made them appraise their own conduct and appreciate the power of forgiveness. If we are faithful to God,
will God be faithful to us? Does God keep his promise?
Meditation: O God, help us as You helped Joseph to put
ourselves in Your care. May the reading of the life of Joseph
strengthen our faith! *Amen.*

February 20
THE DEEP LOVE OF JOSEPH

"His heart yearned for his brother." (Genesis 43:30b) R.V.)
"His bowels did yearn upon his brother." (Genesis 43:30b A.V.)

The Hebrew word "racham" is usually translated bowels and this is the way the authorized version translates it. Joseph was pained within as he remembered the past. He apparently had no contact with the family and now the brothers had come for help. Benjamin had not gone to Egypt on the first trip and he asked about him. The memories of the past unbrotherliness and the implications of the present opportunity to be brotherly overwhelmed him. Love is high and stirs the emotions as well as the mind. The love of Joseph and the distress of his brothers pained him. Even today the stomach is affected in times of severe stress. Parental love and filial love arouse the emotions as well as the mind. What are bowels of mercy?

Meditation: Help us to remember that love at its highest effects the body and mind. The natural way of love brings comfort. When love is divided or unnatural it upsets the person. Help us to keep love active so that suspicion and hatred will flee. Let brotherly love prevail! *Amen.*

February 21
THE BROTHERS ARE RECONCILED

"I am your brother, Joseph, whom you sold . . . for God sent me before you to preserve life." (Genesis 45:4a, 5c)

What a home scene for an artist! The guilt ridden brothers were humiliated. The situation is reversed; the brothers who once humiliated Joseph are now humiliated before Joseph and the Pharaoh. We have to deal with the cosmos whether we want to or not. Sin rebukes the sinner. Envy is replaced with forgiveness. Righteousness is praised and brings gratification. Does the life of Joseph and his forgiveness suggest any of Jesus' teachings?

Meditation: "If a bit of sunshine hits you, After passing of the cloud

If a fit of laughter gets you, And your spine is feeling proud;

Don't forget to up and fling it, At some Soul who's feeling blue

For the moment that you fling it, It's a boomerang to you."

February 22

ANOTHER HOME SCENE

"Then he fell upon his brother Benjamin's neck and wept; and Benjamin wept upon his neck . . . and after that his brother talked with him." (Genesis 45:14)

Guilt had estranged the brothers. Now forgiveness had united and fortified them. The righteous Joseph had become a saviour to those who had rejected and talked of killing him. Now they had learned the height of the love of Joseph and were reminded of God's plan and care. The God of Abraham, Isaac and Jacob had come to their help and had kept His promise. No wonder it is written in the first Psalm, "For the Lord knoweth the way of the righteous but the way of the wicked will perish." (Psalm 1:6) Joseph exemplifies personal trust in God. If you rely on uprightness the love of God will carry you through.

Meditation: Make each life rich through the bonds of parental and filial love. May Joseph who became a saviour to his brothers be an incentive for us to live and to work to save others. Make us stronger than temptation and wiser than the forces of evil! *Amen.*

February 23

JOSEPH INTERPRETS

"And God sent me before you to preserve for you a remnant on earth." (Genesis 45:7)

Joseph had the ability to interpret the Spirit of God. The brothers by their unbrotherliness had broken the covenant. They aimed to destroy Joseph. God kept His part of the covenant and continued to be their God. One cannot contend successfully against God. Joseph sensed his mission and fulfilled it. When men like the brothers plant the seed of slavery they are fomenting a future revolution and dash for freedom. Those who crucify also open the gates for the resurrection.

Meditation: Wrongdoing may delay Your work, O God, but it cannot prevent Your controlling power. Help us to perceive the working and presence of God in history! May we learn Your truths through history! *Amen.*

February 24

WRONGDOING WEAKENS

"If you know any able men among them, put them in charge of my cattle." (Genesis 47:6c)

As deputy governor over the empire of Pharaoh, Joseph seems to have vigor, influence and freedom. He was permitted to be generous to the unfortunate brothers. The question whether or not they were qualified to be efficient herdsmen was an open one. It gives the impression that the brothers were weak or inefficient. They had failed as herdsmen in the famine stricken area of their father. Were they qualified to be herdsmen in Pharaoh's domain? Can it be that the sin of unbrotherliness had created a sense of guilt which had led to physical and possible mental deterioration?

Meditation: Help us to perceive and understand the work and spirit of God at work in history. May my devotion to You be such that any ability I may now possess will not be

taken away. Help me to respect myself by living respectfully
that others may respect me! *Amen.*

February 25
THE BROTHERS BECOME SERVANTS

*"You have saved our lives; may it please my lord, we will be
slaves to Pharaoh."* (Genesis 47:25)

The brothers had sold Joseph to the Ishmaelites (Genesis
37:25-28) or to the Midianites (Genesis 37:28, 36) thinking
that he would be a slave forever. This was a substitute for
shedding his blood by killing him. Later these same men were
humiliated when they became slaves in Egypt. They probably
had no other choice. How often history both religious and
secular has shown that inhuman acts become boomerangs
that fall upon the wrongdoers.

Meditation: Our God, we thank You for the leadership of
Joseph and his willingness to serve, to forgive and to save.
May the lessons that Joseph and his brothers teach show us
the wrongs of unbrotherliness and the consequences. Joseph
kept the convenant but the brothers had not. Help us to
rely on Your promises! *Amen.*

February 26
JOSEPH COMFORTS HIS BROTHERS

*"Joseph said 'you meant evil against me; but God meant it
for good.' "* (Genesis 50:20)

This was Joseph's interpretation of the preceding events.
The evil of the brothers in being unbrotherly impaired their
ability to withstand famine. They may have become frustrated
and were near extinction. Through Joseph the remnant was
saved. God guided Joseph because he was willing to be guided
and now Joseph philosophizes about God's care, goodness and
power. Joseph interprets the ways of God to be rewarding,
whereas the ways of sin brought confusion with guilt and

frustration. Now in this extremity the brothers had to live in the way they made for themselves—the way of slavery. Joseph through his righteousness lived in the ways in which God guided him and in which he was willing to be guided. Do you suppose the reading of the life of Joseph by Jesus had any effect on Jesus' own life?

Meditation: We pray that we may never succumb to evil. If we should fail You and do wrong may we become repentent and turn to righteousness. Make us and keep us as Your faithful children! *Amen.*

February 27
JOSEPH AIDS HIS BROTHERS

"Joseph said . . . 'do not fear; I will provide for you and your little ones.' " (Genesis 50:19a, 21a)

What a contrast in treatment! The brothers thought they had sold Joseph into slavery. What they had expected concerning him came to them. Joseph, however, forgave them, fed them, welcomed and comforted them. He showed no spirit of revenge. The universe or cosmos itself had punished them. The universe does not like unbrotherliness. God is within the cosmos and it is planned for righteousness on the part of His created children. It may be written that the people in Israel never forgot the goodness and power of God to Joseph and the survival of the remnant through him. Joseph overcame evil with good. He became to some extent the progenitor of the teachings of the New Testament. In what ways were Joseph and Jesus alike?

Meditation: O God, we believe that Your covenant with us is still in force. We believe You do not forsake those who do Your will. Keep us faithful! *Amen.*

February 28
HOPE THROUGH GOD WHEN IN BONDAGE

"And Joseph said . . . 'I am about to die; but God will visit you.' " (Genesis 50:24b)

The treachery of the brothers had reacted unfavorably upon them. Joseph tried to bolster their faith and hope before he died. He knew that hard days were ahead. Future Pharaohs and deputy governors would not know their relation to Joseph and they would have unsympathetic taskmasters. Joseph encouraged them never to lose hope or faith in God. The retelling of the faithfulness of Joseph must have been a favorite historical story in the homes of the Israelites and when they gathered around their campfires and their places of worship. Does a later return of the Israelites to the fatherland in Palestine have any relation to Jesus' faith in a resurrection and restoration?

Meditation: Our Father, we have hope for peace, the prevalence of good will and the promotion of righteousness. We have freedom, historical examples, prophetic teachings and the life, death, resurrection and teachings of Jesus to help us to act and to live as free persons with a moral law! *Amen.*

February 29
MOSES IS SAVED TO BE A DELIVERER

"And God said to Moses, I AM WHO I AM.*"* (Exodus 3:14)

Moses was saved, when male babies were unwanted by the Pharaoh, and grew to manhood. Being taught as the Egyptian children and also by his mother he became versed in both the wisdom and customs of the Egyptians and Hebrews. He was disturbed by the hardness of the slave labor of the Hebrews and thought it to be his duty to help them. His exile in Midian was rewarded by the light, warmth and voice of God as it was manifested out of the burning bush. This sight

and insight moved Moses to action. He was convinced that
God cared.

Meditation: Like Moses we know that GOD IS and that he
cares for what He has created. Give us the courage of Moses
to make freedom secure for ourselves and others. May we
accept the evidences within and without ourselves that God is
real and cares what we do! *Amen.*

March 1
MOSES RECEIVES A MESSAGE FROM GOD

*"I have seen the affliction of my people . . . and have heard
their cry . . . I have come down to deliver them."* (Exodus
3:7-8)

Read the first chapters of Exodus about the saving of
Moses, his early education, the theophany of the burning bush
and the plight of the Israelites. You will agree that Moses
is used by God to do a certain work at a specified time. Like
Abraham, he was born at a time when slavery was at its
worst. Moses, like Lincoln, became an agent of God to bring
liberty. God does not like slavery. Even slavery among the
Greeks and Romans did not avail for any lasting good.

Meditation: O God, help us to accept as a truism that You
do not like slavery. Wherever slavery has existed the people
have deteriorated. Since we have learned that slavery and
any addiction to wrong habits deteriorates, let us not support
them. Keep us from habits that harm! *Amen.*

March 2
MOSES RESPONDS TO THE SUPREME BEING

"Say this to the people of Israel, 'I AM has sent me.'" (Exodus 3:14c)

Moses had a twofold duty. First, he was to convince the
Israelites that God meant to deliver them and that he was
God's agent. Second, he was to get the Israelites loosed from

the power of the Egyptians. The united effort and cooperation of the Israelites was necessary. The Israelites in early times seemed to think of God's name being GOD ALMIGHTY. To Moses He was the Supreme Being, "YAHWEH, THE ALL BEING," who had sent him to be a deliverer. Do you think that the teachings of his mother, Jochebed (Exodus 6:20), about the patriarchs had influence upon Moses' spirit and decisions? *Meditation:* Whatever name we apply to God, He is still our God. We should obey His will. As the burning bush became to Moses a revelation of God so may the life and spirit of Jesus as we know it be a revelation to us! *Amen.*

March 3
MOSES' MARCHING ORDERS

"The God of the Hebrews has met with us; let us go." (Exodus 5:3a)

This is what Moses and Aaron were told to tell the Pharaoh. They tried to convince him that they were a covenant people with the SUPREME BEING (YAHWEH) that had been known by the patriarchs as GOD ALMIGHTY. Moses felt that his people had a right to be free. His mission to help them should have convinced Pharaoh that the determination and right to be free was justified and that they deserved to leave peacefully. How can tyrants, who often have been kings, be convinced that people have a right to be free? Could the plagues and frustrations have been avoided if Pharaoh had understood the Hebrew notion of God?

Meditation: Help us to listen to reason and use our intelligence to be considerate of others whether we like it or not. The task of leading persons out of physical or mental bondage is difficult but it is the mission of the church. Help us to release people from the bondage of sin! *Amen.*

March 4
THE COVENANT REMEMBERED

"I have remembered my covenant. I am the Lord and I will bring you out from under the burdens of the Egyptians." (Exodus 6:5c, 6b)

We remember that the SUPREME BEING whom the patriarchs worshipped made a covenant with the Hebrews. The patriarchs believed that God was compassionate and would lead them. Moses undertook the mission of leading the enslaved descendants of the patriarchs to their heritage of liberty under God. The task of being released from the domination of Pharaoh was difficult. The unifying of the people and the method of educating and disciplining them in the ways of freedom had to be devised. Moses had to depend on the guidance of God.

Meditation: May we have persons with the spirit of Moses in every city, hamlet, church and society in our land. We want to be Your people and we pray to be released from bondage, ignorance and misunderstandings! *Amen.*

March 5
THE PEOPLE ACCEPT MOSES

"And the people bowed their heads and worshipped." (Exodus 12:27)

The Israelites had to choose whether they would accept the leadership of Moses or remain under Pharaoh. This privilege of choice has in it the seeds of democracy. Pharaoh was obstinate. Some hardships that he demanded of the Hebrews came upon the Egyptians. There were at least ten plagues. During the period of the plagues the Israelites were worshipping God and reminding themselves that they were a covenant people with a covenant God. This made their worship simple but genuine. The Passover had its origin during this period. God proved Himself to be more powerful than the

gods of the Egyptians. The road to freedom became clearer
and more desirable than the ways of slavery.

Meditation: May we have leaders among us who know God.
Help us to distinguish true leaders from the false! May I be
a true leader like Moses. *Amen.*

March 6
MOSES GIVES ASSURANCE

"Stand firm and see the salvation of the Lord." (Exodus
14:13a)

When the Israelites finally left Egypt and saw the Egyptians
following they became panic-stricken. Moses encouraged them
to press on. The Hebrews had probably surveyed the land
and difficulties in advance and crossed the sea barrier in
safety. The Egyptians probably became frustrated, and in
their haste lacked caution with the result that their chariot
wheels were mired and they were overwhelmed by the water.
The Israelites had safely reached the dry land on the other
side of the sea and were free. They attributed their success to
the guidance of God. They were in their own opinion God-
controlled.

Meditation: O Lord, You are master of the sea, winds, sun
and all that is in them. You are the God of order and power
and worthy of worship. May we always keep Your power in
mind and worship You in spirit and in truth! *Amen.*

March 7
THE SONG OF MOSES

*"The Lord is my strength and song and he has become my
salvation."* (Exodus 15:2a)

This line from the longer poem may have been sung often
by the Israelites. It is part of a very old song. Poetry is more
easily memorized than prose. It suggests the staying power
and accomplishment of God. This fifteenth chapter sings of

the triumph that was won by the might of the spirit of God.
The Hebrews had no physical equipment with which to fight
the Egyptians but they did have faith in the guidance of God.
The desire and need for freedom was on the side of the Hebrews. The above verse is often recited by ministers when
persons unite with the Church or accept the guiding Spirit of
Christ and commit themselves to His service.

Meditation: May we, like Abraham Lincoln, pray that we
are on the side of God. His way is the right way and the highway. If we commit ourselves to God there are resources to
help us just as there were resources to help Moses. May we
always keep on the highway of freedom with love! *Amen.*

March 8
HOW GOD LEADS

*"Thou hast led in thy steadfast love the people whom thou
hast redeemed."* (Exodus 15:13a)

This song of triumph attributed to Moses has staying as
well as steadying values. It is older than the prose literature
with which it is placed. The repetition of this song must have
had devotional value to the people in their trek through the
wilderness as well as for future generations. The release from
slavery and the acceptance of God as their controlling master
reminds us of the incident of a man who once bought a slave
girl at auction and said "Now, you are free." The girl then
said to her former master, "Thank God, and now may I be
your servant?"

Meditation: We know from history and experience that sin
enslaves but that if we sin we have an advocate with the
Father. May sin not overwhelm me as it did the Egyptians!
Amen.

March 9

THE SONG OF MIRIAM

Sing to the Lord, for he has triumphed gloriously." (Exodus 15:21)

This song of Miriam, the sister of Moses, is very old and must have been a source of devotional strength as it was repeatedly sung in the camps, tents and worship services. With the knowledge of triumph in the past they could be more enthusiastic about going forward. As the *Aeneid* by Virgil memorialized the conquest of Troy, so this song of Miriam memorializes the wilderness journey for freedom of the Hebrews. It can hardly be named a battle song although it portrays victory over the enemy. Would this song be a basic thought for some modern hymn?

Meditation: May each day be one of song because of what God has done. Help us to live victoriously in spirit regardless of the physical problems. May no evil dominate us and may every noble virtue cement us! *Amen.*

March 10

MANNA SUSTAINS

"It is the bread which the Lord has given you to eat." (Exodus 16:15c)

New situations strengthen old truths. The long trek from Egypt to Canaan required care and planning. When they camped and planted at a certain place they had to remain in that area until the crops had been gathered. When pasture became scarce they had to move on. On occasions when they were hard pressed God provided manna. They had learned that if they cared for themselves God cared for them. God constantly supplied spiritual manna for them and he is providing it for us now. Douglas MacArthur is reported to have said that "we have gone as far in science as we need to go

until we catch up with the right spirit." Do you believe this
is a correct analysis?
Meditation: As food supports and nourishes the body so may
the spirit with prayer nourish the spirit. May we be aware
that God is constantly giving us the true bread of the Spirit!
Amen.

March 11
MOSES SMITES THE ROCK

*"You shall strike the rock, and water shall come out of it, that
the people may drink."* (Exodus 17:6b)

Water was scarce when the Hebrews camped at Rephidim.
The people became panic-stricken and complained against
Moses. They were almost ready to stone him when the rock
at Horeb yielded water. Why did they not dig and find water
of their own initiative? Why did they depend so much upon
Moses? Had they learned that heaven helps those who help
themselves? Do oil diggers complain and quit when they do
not strike oil or do they dig another well and keep trying? Are
we trying hard enough to keep the springs of freedom flowing?
Meditation: May we depend on God sufficiently by trying
to help ourselves. May we employ our own skills, reason,
brawn and intelligence as we live in this orderly universe! As
we sow and reap let us thank You for the gifts of grace, intelligence and insight! *Amen.*

March 12
JETHRO MEETS MOSES AND IS THANKFUL

*"Jethro said, 'Blessed be the Lord, who hath delivered you
out of the hand of the Egyptians.'"* (Exodus 18:10a)

The meeting of Moses with his father-in-law, Jethro, is a
scene worthy of a great artist. The conversations convinced
Jethro that the God of Moses was greater than all the native
gods. Jethro joined Moses and the people in worshipping the

God of Israel. It is a real achievement when a relative is convinced that the greatest God is the God of Love.

Meditation: We are grateful that Jethro and Moses became comrades in a common cause. Jethro gave considerable help to Moses. May our friends help us to serve, to love and to remain free in Your service! *Amen.*

March 13
JETHRO COUNSELS WITH MOSES

"I will give you counsel, and God be with you." (Exodus 18:19)

Here we have brotherly cooperation at its best. Moses had been teacher, judge, supervisor, etc., and was being overworked. He was showing the strain when Jethro counseled him to devise laws, commandments and directives so that others could decide cases when judgment was needed. The democratic principles needed codification so that others could judge cases and relieve Moses. Jethro may have sown the seed that led to the codification of what we call the Ten Commandments. Democratic people need laws to coordinate their activities. Moses seems to have profited by the advice of Jethro who proved to be a real friend. Is it wise to listen to the advice of others?

Meditation: We thank You, God, for the help of comrades. Men of other cultures are often able to help in difficult situations by sharing their experience and knowledge. May we always remember that we are bound together by common laws of decency! *Amen.*

March 14
LAWS ARE GIVEN

"The people answered together and said, 'All that the Lord hath spoken we will do.'" (Exodus 19:8b)

Some of the people almost regarded Moses as a god. They

accepted his judgment and advice. When he had gone to Mount Sinai and was there a long time, the people again became frustrated. Then when he came down from the mountain with laws the people accepted them and God was again exalted. These laws were needed to remind the people of their part of the covenant. The laws included statements to regulate worship and conduct in human relations. Are the Ten Commandments still to be kept today? Do you know the Commandments which Moses is supposed to have received from God?

Meditation: May the laws that democratic governments make have in them the primary principles that will regulate proper human relations! Let us keep the breath of liberty you gave to mankind pure and holy as You are holy. *Amen.*

March 15

SOME EARLY LAWS

"You shall not make gods of silver to be with me, nor shall you make yourselves gods of gold." (Exodus 20:23)

As the democratic procedures progressed the need for laws and standards of conduct and worship became imperative. Although we do not know definitely what these laws were, yet we do know that the book of the covenant (Exodus 20:22-23:33) contains very ancient laws and standards. This is a good time to read the Ten Commandments for ourselves (Exodus 20:1-17) as well as the book of the covenant. Were the Ten Commandments adequate? Do you think the book of the covenant is older than the Ten Commandments?

Meditation: May Your laws, O God, become our laws, Your ways our ways and Your will our wills! Help us to remember that the Ten Commandments, although negative in form, are still in force. Help me to keep them! *Amen.*

March 16
LEX TALIONIS OR LAW OF RETALIATION

"You shall give life for life, eye for eye, tooth for tooth, hand for hand, foot for foot, burn for burn, wound for wound, stripe for stripe." (Exodus 21:23b-24)

The lex talionis or law of retaliation was a check for primitive savagery. It marks an advance over the custom of limitless revenge. Lamech in Genesis 4:24 claimed the right of limitless revenge, whereas the law of retaliation limits it as "like for like." Do you think the conduct of the patriarchs and Moses had influence in lessening the ways of revenge and the notion that it is the duty of the injured to injure without limit? While the "lex talionis" is far from being Christian, yet it is an advance over previous social laws that sanctioned cruelty and revenge without limit. Through the "like for like" system we note in our study that the Spirit of man is becoming more lenient.

Meditation: We are grateful for the courts. Let us pray for the judges that they may seek justice in dealing with unsocial persons. We are thankful that Jesus taught the high law of the Spirit! *Amen.*

March 17
THE LAW OF BLOOD REVENGE

"Whoever sheds the blood of man, by man shall his blood be shed." (Genesis 9:6)

The law of blood revenge is apparently an outgrowth of the kinship of the tribe. Any injury to a member of the tribe meant that other members of the tribe were duty bound to avenge the injury. Cain had no tribal protector and when he cried to God for protection it was thought that God protected him. God intervened in caring for those whom he had created when there were no persons to help. Do you think that "lex talionis" and the "law of blood revenge" were formulated before or after the Ten Commandments? Although these laws limit cruelty and revenge, yet they are far from the Christian principles of Righteousness.

Meditation: May all people accept and use the Spirit of the living God and be orderly in all their ways. May we develop the spirit of good will so that all acts of revenge may be completely outmoded! *Amen.*

March 18
GOD'S PROMISE RECALLED

"Remember . . . to whom thou didst swear by thine own self, and didst say to them, 'I will multiply your descendants as the stars of heaven.' " (Exodus 32:13bc)

The Israelites were a difficult group to manage. The years of slavery had not made them self-reliant. The absence of Moses on the mountain gave them an opportunity to revert to material images of worship and they built a golden calf, and worshipped it. This idea of a golden calf and unsocial conduct was probably copied from the conduct of the pagan neighbors. In a spirit of repentance they recalled the promise of God and became aware again that there is no self or image greater than God and each self is most like God when keeping the laws and commandments.

Meditation: Help us to realize that mankind is a creature of time and has made progress in proper social conduct slowly. Work, O God, Yourself into us so that each of us will do Your will. *Amen.*

March 19
MOSES DEMANDS A DECISION

"Who is on the Lord's side? Come to me." (Exodus 32:26b)

Because of the sin of the golden calf the people were spiritually naked. A riot occurred. Many persons were slain. The golden calf incident reads like heathen influence at work among the Israelites rather than the actions of people who had a covenant with a creative God. To advance and maintain social decorum it may have been necessary to eliminate a group of the misguided. Why did they reject God's covenant and God Himself who had helped them to freedom? Although many were slain, yet a remnant remained who were loyal to a covenant God; these regarded God as a Spirit and not in the image of a calf.

Meditation: Save us from error in judgement. May we build rather than destroy the power and might of God's plan. Keep us aware that we are Your children. We have a covenant to obey. Break down every semblance of idolatry! *Amen.*

March 20

MOSES IS SHOWN THE GRACIOUSNESS OF GOD

"I will be gracious to whom I will be gracious, and will show mercy on whom I will show mercy." (Exodus 33:19c)

The reading of this portion of Scripture seems to portray Moses as being confused about the nature of God in that he asked to see God's glory. Maybe the disastrous plagues in Egypt and the fickleness of the people in building and worshipping the golden calf worried him. He had thought of God as powerful and gracious. Here God reveals Himself as gracious to those who obey and harsh to the disobedient. The nature of the universe as gracious to the gracious and obedient, and severe to the wicked and disobedient, had to be learned. It seems to be a truth that wickedness destroys and righteousness edifies. This philosophy of the universe is clear.

Meditation: May we conduct ourselves so the gracious God can help us. To worship other than a gracious God with gracious and merciful acts is to substitute another god for that of Abraham and Joseph. May we be assured that truth will triumph! *Amen.*

March 21

THE NATURE OF GOD

"A God merciful and gracious, slow to anger, and abounding in steadfast love and faithfulness." (Exodus 34:6)

This text is further assurance to Moses that the graciousness and compassion of God to the patriarchs was consistent with His nature. God is dependable, gracious and forgiving to the gracious and forgiving but harsh to the unthankful and wicked. This is a moral law of the universe. This moral law is as dependable in the realm of the spirit as the law of gravity is dependable in the physical universe. We may be assured that this is an orderly universe and that God will keep His part of the covenant. Will we keep our part of the covenant? Did the people of Israel keep their part of the covenant? If we keep the covenant and assume and accept God we will know God but if not then He will be to us a mystery.

Meditation: Since You are gracious we should also be gracious to You and to all people. May we keep Your Spirit active among us by being gracious, forgiving and doers of Your will! *Amen.*

March 22

THE COVENANT

"I have made a covenant with you and with Israel." (Exodus 34:27b)

The ritual decalogue may have been a part of a Kenite decalogue. It may have been carved on stone. These laws have been valuable in teaching the nature of God and the simple worship that He required. For the sake of the people the worship of God was essential. As long as the people kept the laws the tent was a sufficient covering and place of worship. God did not delight in sacrifice but in sacrificial service. Do you think that these early ritual laws contained the gist of the Ten Commandments? Were the Ten Commandments embodied in these laws? The wilderness was a place of trial and decision.

Meditation: You are constantly renewing the covenant with us. We continually transgress but You are merciful, kind and forgiving. It is our will that You should reign and control us by Your Spirit. *Amen.*

March 23

THE WHOLENESS OF GOD

"You shall be holy; for I the Lord your God am holy." (Leviticus 19:2b)

Chapters seventeen to twenty-six in the book of Leviticus preserve for us the "holiness code" and in this nineteenth chapter we have the nature of God as holy and the need for man to love his neighbor as himself. (Leviticus 19:18d) Do you think the "holiness of God" implies the wholeness of God? From the idea of God's completeness may have evolved the notion of "holiness" in the sense of sacredness and thence was spelled "holy" instead of "wholly." We like to think of God as complete and that His plan is complete for us. Up to this time no one seems to have devised a better directive of society than that of the "moral order."

Meditation: Keep me wholly Thine and Your holiness and wholeness will keep me holy. May Your completeness bring all people to love and obey Your will. May we continue to sing "Holy, Holy, Holy, Lord God Almighty, merciful and mighty." *Amen.*

March 24

RIGHTEOUS JUDGMENT REQUIRED

"You shall do no injustice in judgment." (Leviticus 19:15a)

In this code righteousness is the standard of judgment. Revenge, jealousy, envy and hatred should not prevail and influence judgment. A judge should know righteousness to effect justice. The aim of the "holiness code" was to help people get along well with neighbors and others. To follow the "holiness code" is to make no discrimination as to race, color or creed. Only character stands forth as a basis of judgment. Jesus may have read and reread this "holiness code" in that he embodied much of it in his teaching and conduct. It may have helped to construct his philosophy.

Meditation: Let no prejudice, jealousy, envy or hatred make us unfair to others in word or in deed. May security for others be as sacred to them as it is to ourselves! *Amen.*

March 25
A PART OF THE GREAT COMMANDMENT

"You shall love your neighbor as yourself." (Leviticus 19:18c)

This positive commandment was not overlooked by Jesus. It is one of the highlights for morality in both Testaments. Lamech and others had justified their actions of revenge, vengeance and cruelty in order to justify their own power and satisfy their own thirst for vengeance. The holiness code does not justify this sort of conduct but suggests "love for a neighbor," as a proper mode of conduct. This demands the same respect for another person that one has for himself. We should treat others as we would wish to be treated. Each person as an individual should be positive and outgoing with human and divine concerns. To "love a neighbor as oneself" requires intelligence. To judge a neighbor requires the ability to put one's self in his situation.

Meditation: We were created with Your breath in us and Your spirit. Let us remember that we are persons who deal and live with persons. May we have the same respect for others that we have for ourselves! *Amen.*

March 26
LOVE TOWARD A STRANGER

"When a stranger sojourns with you . . . you shall love him as yourself." (Leviticus 19:33ae, 34b)

A neighbor may not always be an Israelite but the same standard of morality and forgiveness should be shown even if he is a stranger. God had led the Israelites into freedom and He is also concerned that others should be free, therefore one should not be discriminatory. This law about the treatment of a stranger may have come later than the rule of "love thy neighbor as thyself."

Meditation: We thank You, God, that You guided Jesus in making this law of neighborliness a positive norm of action. May it continue to challenge our intelligence and be operative so often that it will become intuitive! Help us to grasp and to understand the value of the self! *Amen.*

March 27
UNRIGHTEOUS JUDGMENT FORBIDDEN

"You shall do no wrong in judgment." (Leviticus 19:35a)

Love toward a neighbor and stranger should extend into the economic field as well as the social and religious. Righteousness means the doing of that which is right. Doing wrong may be an effort to justify an inner wrong or to satisfy inwardly a wrong done by another. This is never right. We are intelligent persons and we should think as we act and speak. We are not given life to push one another around depending as do the animals upon relative strength. We are created with a spark of divinity. This spark may be a light to guide us always.

Meditation: May we never exult in an occasional clever act or unjust deed of any kind. Cleverness will be weak when placed along side of godliness. May my transactions be open, fair and with a sense of justice! *Amen.*

March 28

CONSECRATE YOURSELF

"Consecrate yourselves, therefore, and be holy." (Leviticus 20:7a)

Sanctification and consecration describe ethics in practice. They sanction the elements of common decency. Ritual may help to cleanse the mind. Water may wash the body, but to keep the mind and body clean requires constant thought vigilance. The laws of society have become many but the basic laws of living righteously are simple.

Meditation: May we constantly purify our minds with prayer, meditation, noble thinking and Your will. May nothing be too hard or too inconvenient when it is the right thing to do. Keep us wholly Thine! *Amen.*

March 29

DEFILE NOT YOURSELF

"You shall not lie carnally with your neighbor's wife and defile yourself with her." (Leviticus 18:20)

This directive points to a time when the sanctity and purity of the family was being developed. The family was regarded as holy and should be kept sacred and complete within itself. To be carnal and defile another is to defile oneself. The self is the highest individual possession; a gift of God's plan of creation and it should be kept clean, pure and holy. The family has replaced the tribe. Even in primitive times tribes were kept intact as this was thought to give strength and prestige in contending with other tribes. Now that the family has come into prominence purity is important and defilement is sin. Is the family the highest unit of happiness today?

Meditation: We are grateful for the commandments, statutes, codes and laws that have been recorded. May we reach a stage in human society when all shall do and think ways of

rightness that will keep the family as a unit of happiness.
Amen!

March 30
DEALING WITH THE WICKED

*"When a man causes a disfigurement . . . fracture for fracture,
eye for eye, tooth for tooth; he has disfigured a man, he shall
be disfigured."* (Leviticus 24:19a, 20)

How to deal with the cruel and unsocial is always a problem. The method of stoning a recalcitrant member was crude
and unmerciful. The thought behind the practice was that
the thought of punishment would reduce wrong acts. The
roots of this method still exist. Sometimes it is spoken of as
a feud. Although the "love and forgiving" emphasis existed,
yet it was not sufficiently accepted to be generally practiced.
Here and there persons would return to the "revenge unlimited" or the "like for like" method. Did it require the
death and resurrection of Jesus to implement the power of
love and forgiveness? Is there vicarious suffering as well as
vicarious joy?

Meditation: Let the right hand of friendship prevail in me
now and always! *Amen.*

March 31
WRONG TO ANOTHER IS FORBIDDEN

"You shall not wrong one another." (Leviticus 25:17a)

As the early laws are laid side by side they are inconsistent.
We have to distinguish periods of time and culture. We also
have to compare the laws made by kings and secular society
with those made within the field of religion. We have to keep
in mind that while God is thought of by some as a God of
vengeance He is also thought of by others as a God of love.
We must remember that love does no wrong to another. Love
does not assume the prerogative of vengeance which belongs

to God. Love accepts God as Love and does not make a God of the self. The self is the gift of God and human beings should protect the self with good.

Meditation: Help us to stay human in all our ways. We want to do our duty within the moral law but we do not presume to judge the ways of others. May we join with Jesus in thinking that God is love and that loves does no harm to another. *Amen.*

April 1

SINS ARE PUNISHABLE

"I will smite you, even I, sevenfold for your sins, and I will bring a sword upon you, that shall execute vengeance for the covenant." (Leviticus 26:24b-25a)

The nature of God is Love. Like gravity it is orderly in operation. Sin, which is missing the mark of doing right, is associated with impurities and wrongdoing. Since God has made a covenant with man it was conceded by some that sin itself would punish the wrongdoer as often as seven times and that God would have mercy and forgive the sinner seven times. The hurt for disobeying the moral law is commensurate with the hurt in disobeying the physical law of gravity. How do you think that we are punished for our sins today? Is guilt a signal that we should seek and accept the forgiveness of God and those whom we may have wronged?

Meditation: Mankind has sought in many ways through history to punish and help the wrongdoer. Many of them have been futile and misdirected. Help us to accept love with forgiveness as the proper method! *Amen.*

April 2

GOD WILL REMEMBER THE COVENANT

"I will remember my covenant." (Leviticus 26:42)

If the way of love and righteousness prevailed mankind

would be free. All would work for the good of all. The aim of each person would be to develop his own personality and that of every other person. When the covenant with God is broken by man, men blame one another. Sin brings disorder to the mind, the body and society. The sinner by his or her own conduct loses favor with God and the cosmos that He created. The covenant suggests that every person can and should function in an orderly fashion just as the physical world does. May it be true that a scientist can tell the exact location of a planet at a certain time but cannot tell the location of his own daughter at twelve o'clock midnight?

Meditation: Eternal God, our Father, may I begin this day with new expectations and hopes of helping to build a friendly and fraternal world order beginning with myself! *Amen.*

April 3

THE AARONIC BENEDICTION

"The Lord bless you and keep you; The Lord be gracious to you . . . and give you peace." (Numbers 6:24-26)

This benediction is in keeping with the patriarchial idea of God's concern and care. The graciousness of God and the personal manifestation of Himself should help us to have inward and outward peace. This benediction is given today in many churches and places. It has been repeated through the centuries. Are we in danger today of losing God among the material stuff and forfeiting his blessings?

Meditation: May we find You in the spirit of man. May material possessions be used to shelter the bodies of mankind. May we be as worthy of Your blessings as was Joseph. May we, like Joseph, become a saviour to some even if others of our fellowmen become slaves to wrong habits! *Amen.*

April 4

GOD CARRIED HIS PEOPLE

"You have seen what I did to the Egyptians, and how I bore you on eagles' wings and brought you to myself." (Exodus 19:4)

This endearing sentence is a reminder of the way that God led the people from slavery in Egypt into freedom. God was intimate and carried them as an eagle carries her young from one place to another. They had the sayings and traditions of the patriarchs when in Egypt but now they had God for themselves. The wilderness journey gave them a sense of the intimacy and power of God and with these ideas of God came laws, commandments, courage, faith, victory, the fulfillment and renewal of the covenant and above all the consciousness of God Himself being with them.

Meditation: Our Father, You are always doing good things to and for us. Your provident care includes the gift of mind, body and spirit of Yourself in us. May we be worthy of Your care! *Amen.*

April 5

THE PROTECTING CLOUD

"Thou goest before them, in a pillar of cloud by day and in a pillar of fire by night." (Numbers 14:14d)

This is another statement that arose about the care and leading of the people. A cloud hovered over them in the daytime to protect and warm them just as a bird hovers over her young to protect and warm the little ones. God was just as solicitous in leading and helping them at night with a pillar of fire. He did not forsake or neglect them day or night. Once while in slavery they were as no people but now they had become a people with initiative, purpose, mission and the consciousness of a protecting God.

Meditation: Let our remembrance of Your care never forsake us. The stream of care that God showed the patriarchs had now come upon them. When I am in a wilderness of indecision send a cloud or light to guide me in the way that is right! May the glow and warmth of Your Holy Spirit hover over me! *Amen.*

April 6
WHEN MOSES WAS DISTURBED

"Carry them in your bosom, as a nurse carries the suckling child." (Numbers 11:12b)

Moses was disturbed because the people were so helpless. They lacked initiative and were so dependent upon him to help them in their problems that he came and talked it over with the Lord, asking if he should continue to carry them and coddle them as a father does a baby. It was made known that a better organization was needed, with the result that seventy persons were briefed about responsibilities and principles. The spirit of leadership that was with Moses was given to them, with the result that they learned to talk with God and were willing to be guided by God just as Moses had been. Was this time of discouragement and its solution a basis for the development of our democratic way of life, when each person may talk with God and be responsible for his own religion and citizenship?

Meditation: We rejoice that some among us have the Spirit of God to impart and to share. May more of our church men and women be receptive to Your guiding Spirit and assume initiative and leadership! *Amen.*

April 7
MORE PROPHETS NEEDED

"Would that all the Lord's people were prophets, and that the Lord would put his spirit upon them." (Numbers 11:29b)

Moses was a statesman and a prophet. Among the seventy

men that became imbued with the spirit of God were Eldad and Medad. They failed to share in the briefing but became active in prophesying. This disturbed Joshua and the matter was brought to Moses who said, "Would that all the Lord's people were prophets," etc. Was it possible that Joshua had needlessly become disturbed? Might Joshua or some of the others have become jealous? In many cases Moses did not curb them. Moses was inclusive and welcomed any who had the spirit of God to help. He made them feel that they, too, had a mission as well as talent to discharge it.

Meditation: Give us Your Spirit, O God, that we may discern good and evil! *Amen.*

April 8

MOSES INTERCEDED

"Pardon the iniquity of this people, I pray thee, according to the greatness of thy steadfast love." (Numbers 14:19a)

Moses thought that God's leadership should have kept them loyal, faithful, thankful and responsive regardless of hardships. Instead of being appreciative they were impatient, and murmured so that Moses finally interceded for them. Should they have pitched in and helped Moses instead of taking time out of his busy schedule? Moses knew it was the nature of God to forgive and he acted the part of a priest. Can a man be a priest as well as a prophet? Can a person be a prophet and not a priest? Are the ministers you know both priests and prophets? The people in this case should have gone directly to God. They should have been their own priests.

Meditation: Help us to keep courageous in the midst of adversity! In case others with whom we work are weak and indifferent, may our intercessory prayers for them be answered! *Amen.*

April 9

THE SUPPORTING POWER

"The Lord is with us." (Numbers 14:9)

There were major and minor reports from the spies who had gone ahead to see the land of Canaan. The majority reported that the land was already possessed and that there were many obstacles in the way. The minority report by Joshua and Caleb was that they should proceed and that the natives of the land would help them and that they should be friendly to them. Moses joined in thinking that the people of the land would help them with food and that God would continue to help them, and therefore they should proceed to possess the land. Do you think the faith of Moses was justified?

Meditation: The great boon of mankind is the possibilities of freedom with God. May we have intelligence and ability to use the land we have and keep the freedom that You and our fathers have given to us! *Amen.*

April 10

GOD IS WORKING

"What has God wrought." (Numbers 23:23d)

Belaam was a prophet who consistently prophesied good in behalf of Israel. He was aware of the covenant relationship and believed that God was working for Israel. Balak, king of Moab, tried to bribe him to prophesy evil against Israel but he stood firm and would not change. Balaam evidently had considerable influence in that he heard the words of the Lord and could only speak good concerning Israel's future. We still hold that God is working for the welfare of all people and that this is God's world and that He will care for it. He continues to supply air, water, time, light, soil, life and mind to people. Science accepts the fact that the universe is orderly and mysterious.

Meditation: O God, we thank You that You continue to move in an orderly and mysterious way in the performance of Your wonderful universe of matter and of mind. Let both continue to be important and necessary for our well-being! *Amen.*

April 11
GOD'S CARE FOR ISRAEL

"He found him in a desert land . . . he encircled him, he cared for him, he kept him as the apple of his eye." (Deuteronomy 32:10)

This is another ancient poem attributed to Moses showing the intimate concern of God. It may have been sung often at the campfires and in the sacred assemblies. This verse praises God for his watchful care while bringing Israel through the wilderness and in keeping them free and moving forward. It portrays God finding Israel as if it were an abandoned child. He cared for it, kept it in his mind and watched it as if it were the apple of his eye. He was like a nursing father to Israel. Israel should be a dutiful child.

Meditation: May the constant repetition of God's care for Israel help us to appreciate His care for us. As we find satisfaction in the achievements of our own children so, we believe, You rejoice over us when we are righteous, appreciative and worshipful. Make us worthy of YOURSELF! *Amen.*

April 12
GOD TAUGHT ISRAEL

"As an eagle that stirs up its nest, that flutters over its young." (Deuteronomy 32:11a)

When the eagle teaches the eaglets to fly she begins by showing the strength and stability in flight of her own wings. She even carries the little ones in safety to great heights. She has to teach them the power of their own wings, and there are times when the parent eagle will push the young from the nest so the eaglets will use their own wings. God, according to this song, taught Israel to be self-reliant, self-sufficient and self-responsible. God wants us to do our part in living in a world where righteousness may prevail. Am I, as an individual, and are we, as people of a nation, living up to the intent for which we were created?

Meditation: If I am afraid to use my own resources then chastise me and treat me roughly so that I may learn to help myself with righteousness and trust. May Your care be an incentive for my concern and care for others! *Amen.*

April 13
GOD LITERALLY CARRIED ISRAEL

"He spread abroad his wings, catching them, bearing them on its pinions." (Deuteronomy 32:11bc)

God did not want his covenant people to remain in thraldom. He stirred them up so that they were willing to leave Egypt and have freedom. He taught them in the wilderness how to make laws and use them, how to sustain themselves and how to make progress toward their objective. Through experience they learned how to live together, how to worship together and how to work together. They discovered when they appraised the journey that God's concern for them should inspire them to care for others through exemplary conduct.

Meditation: Make me self-sufficient through Your efficiency. May I know how to take care of myself for then I can best care for and help others! *Amen.*

April 14
A STUDY OF THE VENGEANCE OF GOD

"Vengeance is mine, and recompense." (Deuteronomy 32:35a)

The search to establish justice when wrong has been done has long been a problem. We have seen that there were times when men were vengeful without limit. Then, later, this was mitigated by the law of blood revenge, and still later the "like for like" system of vengeance was adopted. This song holds that God is His own avenger and that this is within His creative plan. When men attempt to justify wrongdoing by taking vengeance it leads to further need for vengeance. There is no stopping place. For God to be the vindicator is more in keeping with His complete knowledge, complete care and complete justice and love. The cosmos, according to history, has exalted righteousness and the righteous and denounced and debased the wicked. It has required many centuries of history to teach man that vengeance is a matter for God and not man.

Meditation: If we love God and man completely there is no place for revenge. If our neighbor is not responsive to right and to neighborliness it is his own weakness and our strength. In any situation we will keep being neighborly. Help us to love even the unresponsive person! *Amen.*

April 15
THE HIGHEST REVELATION

"The eternal God is your dwelling place, and underneath are the everlasting arms." (Deuteronomy 33:27)

What height of thought in this poetic statement! The everlasting arms are underneath God's children just as a parent's arms are strong and dependable when holding a child. Parental arms are strong arms that will sacrifice the body itself rather than fail to support the dependant child. God's arms are the everlasting arms.

Meditation: You are ever with us to support us. Persons have been edified in Your presence. May nations and individuals depend on Your everlasting arms for eternal security. *Amen.*

April 16

ISRAEL EXULTS

"Happy are you, O Israel! Who is like you, a people saved by the Lord." (Deuteronomy 33:29ab)

The song of the blessing of Moses seems to hold that Israel would not have survived had it not been for the care of God as it was embodied in the covenant. God shielded some, fed some, led some and guided some. He kept a remnant steadfast and loyal when pagan religious sects were their neighbors. The gods of Baal and the worshippers of Baal did not divert them. This message of appreciation is similar to the witness of many people as they worship. It is better to thank God for what we have than to curse him for what we do not have. God was their saviour and to him a remnant responded and the members of this group were happy.

Meditation: There are 'isms, O God, that attract some people away from You and Your righteousness. Help me to follow Your way for it has been tested and proved by Israel. May the faithful remnant continue its faithfulness! *Amen.*

April 17

GOD'S LOVE IS THE EXPLANATION

"Yea, he loved his people." (Deuteronomy 33:3a)

This is the explanation of God's integrity. His Love never fails. People that turn to other gods find them weak, inefficient and ineffectual. The disloyal to God became lost to Israel because they became lost to themselves. When people do not respect the Love of God they lose respect for their own love. God's Love proved to be real, vital and strong and it is real, strong and vital to the Christian followers today. Do you love God as you should?

Meditation: May we never attempt to forsake God, for we people of other faiths our own faith is confirmed. When we walk in God's step we find Him to be a true leader and guide.

May our love and service to You grow more vital in its use!
Amen.

April 18
FAITHFULNESS OF THE FAITHFUL

"They observed thy word, and kept thy covenant." (Deuteronomy 33:9cd)

The effective prayers of the righteous availeth much. An appreciable remnant of the Israelites had kept the word and the covenant. Through their faithfulness the whole nation of Israel was kept from extinction. In like manner a faithful minority might have saved Sodom and Gomorrah. The unfaithful were kept from annihilation by the faithfulness of the faithful. There were times when the faithful suffered and were delayed by the disloyalty and sins of the unfaithful. Nations and families were bound together and when the disloyal sin the faithful suffer also. The reverse is true also, that when the faithful do right the unfaithful are supported by them. Is there such a thing as vicarious progress and may there also be a vicarious delay?

Meditation: Help us to realize how closely we are bound together. Economics are factors in every society. Religion binds and unites for safety in the ratio of its obedience and purity. Help us to be truly religious! *Amen.*

April 19

HE CARED FOR ISRAEL

"He encompasses him all the day long, and makes his dwelling between his shoulders." (Deuteronomy 33:12cd)

The tribe of Benjamin was well located for safety. It was good imagination for the poet to think of God covering the tribe of Benjamin as a child is covered with a garment. The intimacy of God had been accentuated. It sustained the Israelites even when they were without priest or prophet and each person had to be his or her own priest and prophet.

Meditation: May we never attempt to forsake God, for we know that He will not forsake us. Care for us as we care for our children! May our love and sacrificial service be positive, constant and genuine! *Amen.*

April 20
THE INHABITANTS OF THE LAND

"As I have dealt kindly with you, you also will deal kindly with my father's house." (Joshua 2:12bc)

Rahab and others had heard of the Israelites and their objective. When the spies came to her house in Jericho she received them with kindness but pledged them to return the kindness when they had taken the city. This idea of "like for like" in kindness would be in keeping with the woman and the types of people in the land. Her tenets of belief and character supported her risk in hiding the messengers and in this case it paid off, for when Jericho was captured her house was not harmed. It seems evident that the reputation of the Israelites in having the leadership and care of God had preceded them to the land of Canaan.

Meditation: Have we learned, our Father, that we should be kind and helpful in a righteous cause whether there is a reward offered or not. May our motives be upright and righteous! *Amen.*

April 21
IT IS A DUTY TO BE STRONG

"Be strong and of good courage; be not frightened, neither be dismayed; for the Lord your God is with you wherever you go." (Joshua 1:9bc)

Both history and tradition hold that Moses gave the above instruction and that it was supported by Joshua. The entrance into Canaan was not easy. There was strong resistance but when God leads us and we do His will there is nothing impossible. It was only by being strong, courageous and obedient that God could bring success to them with a minimum of loss. *Meditation:* This parting message of Moses, supported by Joshua in a crisis, may be a message to me. If I smile others may smile but if I lose faith others may falter. Keep me courageous and faithful in going forward! *Amen.*

April 22
HEAR THE WORDS OF THE LORD

"Come hither, and hear the words of the Lord your God." (Joshua 3:9)

The book of Joshua in some places does not make the best reading. Exploits and experiences of people in conflict are not always complimentary to the Israelites. Both Moses and Joshua had their troubles with disloyalties and backsliding. It is likely that the customs and amusements of the people of the land were glamorous but not helpful to the Israelite youth. The ways of the secular world often seem more attractive than the ways of God, but they are temporary and less stable. Joshua and Moses felt that the people should worship God, keep the commandments and remain loyal to the God that cared for them and led them into freedom.
Meditation: May each of us fulfill our individual mission whatever that may be. Give us the outreach of Moses, the courage of Joshua and the faithfulness of Caleb! *Amen.*

April 23
JERICHO FALLS

"Joshua said . . . shout; for the Lord hath given you the city." (Joshua 6:16c)

That there was the city of Jericho in the time of Joshua

seems to be a fact of history. The inhabitants worshipped deities other than God. The author is successful in showing the value of faith in God over against the weak elements that controlled the minds of the people in primitive times. The pattern by which Jericho fell is less important than the knowledge that it was destroyed and that the inhabitants worshipped other gods than Jehovah.

Meditation: Let us not become lost in detail as we read the chapters in Joshua. Let us remember that wickedness weakens and destroys and that the people of Jericho were wicked. May we carry the ark of God always with us and worship God and not the ark itself! *Amen.*

April 24

THE LOVE TO GOD IS DEMANDED

"Take good heed to yourselves, therefore, to love the Lord your God." (Joshua 23:11)

We may get the impression as we read the book of Joshua that the God of the Hebrews was a battle-god who favored the Israelites. The destruction of the cities and the wars with the people of the land tended to give the impression that all the people of the land were destroyed. This, however, was an exaggeration. Many of the inhabitants of the land survived and their ways and customs continued to create difficulties for the Hebrews. The temptation of the Hebrews to accept native gods was always present. The Hebrew people were taught about the covenant with God and that they should be loyal. Will God protect and care for those who dishonor Him by wrongdoing and substitute other gods for Him?

Meditation: In hours of victory we need to exercise caution lest pride, false ambition, secularism, materialism, fascism, etc., be substituted for the worship of the God of righteousness and love. Help us to remember that God likes loyalty to Him and self respect in each person! *Amen.*

April 25
THE PEOPLE WITNESS OF THEIR
FAITH IN GOD

"The people said, . . . 'The Lord our God we will serve, and his voice we will obey.' " (Joshua 24:24)

Because Joshua sensed the temptation of the people to accept the gods of Canaan, he repeated the deeds of God in bringing them out of slavery into freedom. He urged them to remember that they were a covenant people who should obey and serve God. A stone was set up as a sanctuary and a witness to their covenant. Joshua taught that the salvation of the people depended upon their obedience to God who loved and cared for them. Joshua must have been heartened when the people resolved to serve and obey.

Meditation: May love guide every act in my life today. When I pray for myself I will also pray for others. May I not be led to feel that God will break cosmic laws for me. Help me to obey God's laws! *Amen.*

April 26
LOVE GIVES WARMTH AND LIGHT

"Let them that love him be as the sun when he goeth forth in his might." (Judges 5:31b A.V.)

The Song of Deborah was very old, crude and primitive. It described how Sisera, a Cannanite army captain, was killed by a woman named Jael. The concluding verse, in the authorized version, seems different from the preceding verses. This verse is more in keeping with later writings in that it indicates that love has power, light, warmth and universality rather than warlike contentions. Could it be that a late editor with a deep concept of the power of God was disturbed by the contents of the Song and added a modern and more positive thought of the nature of God?

Meditation: We are grateful that the Song of Deborah has

been preserved because it shows the conduct and problems of people who did not know the God of the Hebrews as one of love, compassion and power. *Amen.*

April 27

GIDEON IS CALLED

"Peace be to you; do not fear, you shall not die." (Judges 6:23)

When Joshua died the Midianites became aggressive. Gideon became concerned for the safety of the Israelites and prayed for help and was assured by communicating with God that there was no need for fear. Then Gideon began to break down the altars of Baal and to rebuild the former altars of the Israelites. In combatting the enemies, Gideon selected brave and trusted men. The people of Israel were united under Gideon with the result that battles were won by the Israelites and the worship of God was restored. Gideon was assured and he was able to convince the people, that God was with them and that he would keep the covenant. As a Christian would you approve all the methods of Gideon?

Meditation: May we, like Gideon, speak to You before beginning any important mission! May we get rid of everything that weakens morals. Let us build constructively toward a healthy family life for all people! *Amen.*

April 28

GOD IS REGARDED AS THE RULER

"The Lord will rule over you." (Judges 8:23c)

Gideon was willing to be an agent of God. In his campaign Gideon relied on God and communicated with Him as well as with the people. When the Medianites had been defeated the people asked Gideon to rule. Gideon declined on the grounds that God was their ruler and in this way he turned the minds of the people away from the gods of the land to the God of Israel. The attitude of Gideon in selecting the help of strong persons to support his plan may well add another link in the chain of democracy. God, working through Gideon and the loyal Israelites, was thought of as the ruler. Peace followed the victory over the Midianites who in their condescension became cooperative.

Meditation: As Gideon subdued the Midianites with three hundred trusted and disciplined Israelites supported by the Spirit of God, so may we have faithful friends to join in the contention of the forces of evil. *Amen.*

April 29
WICKEDNESS DESTROYS THE WICKED

"And God also made the wickedness of the men of Shechem fall back upon their heads." (Judges 9:57)

Abimelech succeeded his father, Gideon. To make himself secure he slew seventy brothers on one stone. Only Jotham, another brother, survived. Then a rebellion followed and Shechem was destroyed. Abimelech fled to Thebez and besieged it. While trying to take the tower into which many of the natives had fled, a woman threw a millstone on Abimelech that fractured his skull. In desperation he required that one of the young men should kill him so that it could not be said that he had been slain by a woman. The moral is that Abimelech, in slaying his seventy brothers, had sinned and that God found a way to requite the crime. God was the avenger. This is in keeping with the verse in Deuteronomy 32:35, "Vengeance is mine" saith the Lord and the people were beginning to learn that cruelty does not assure safety.

Meditation: May the record of this experience of Abimelech teach us that God does not like injustice for the sake of a presumed idea of safety. The cruelty of Abimelech proved to be a boomerang. May we seek good always! *Amen.*

April 30

A PRIMITIVE VOW

"And Jephthah made a vow to the Lord." (Judges 11:30a)

We have already noted that the inhabitants of the land had a deteriorating influence upon the Israelites. Jephthah was a warrior who, when the Ammonites attacked, was called back from the land of Tob to lead in the defense of Israel. He vowed that he would sacrifice the first person of his own house that met him after he had won victory over the Ammonites. The first person from his house that he saw after the victory was his daughter, an unmarried daughter over whom he had life and death control. He kept his vow and sacrificed his daughter, but the Israelites were not pleased with such a sacrifice of a human being. Does God delight in human sacrifice? Was this the end of human sacrifice among the Hebrews?

Meditation: May we be careful about our promises to God. We do not believe we should make rash promises. May we be careful so that an intended good may not become an evil. May we always promise to build personality! *Amen.*

May 1

LOVE SHARES WITH THE LOVED

"You only hate me, you do not love me." (Judges 14:16b)

These are the words of Samson's wife. Samson, a judge in Israel, had proposed a riddle and had offered a prize to his men friends if one of them could answer it correctly. The Philistine friends of Samson's wife conspired to find out the answer, and the above words seemed to have been a ruse to have Samson tell her the answer. After the wife had told the Philistine friends the answer, they proposed their answer in a riddle to Samson. Their riddle was "What is sweeter than honey? What is stronger than a lion?" The answer is LOVE, for the Philistine men knew the power of love. Samson on account of his love for his wife had told her the answer.

This incident shows that even in times of stress, love is a force.

Meditation: May we realize the power of parental, marital and filial love! Help us to keep love clean, pure and holy in all its phases. May the persistence of parental, marital and filial love keep alive our love to You! *Amen.*

May 2
FEIGNED LOVE WEAKENS

"How can you say, I love you, when your heart is not with me?" (Judges 16:15)

Samson had superior strength. His dedication to God was the source and his long Nazarite hair was the sign. His principle of action seems to have been "like for like" or unlimited revenge upon his enemies. The Philistines with whom he was in conflict wanted to spy out the source of his strength. Samson consorted with Delilah, a loose Philistine woman who wormed from Samson that the secret of his strength was in his hair. She informed the leaders of the Philistines, conjured to cut off Samson's hair and accepted the bribe money. When the Philistines attacked, Samson was weak and was captured. It seems clear that the motive of action on Samson was revenge. Delilah was leagued with the Philistines when she pretended to love Samson. Was Delilah a deceiver as one might expect? Did Samson place his love with the wrong woman? Was Samson mentally weak before the hair was shaven?

Meditation: May we deplore lust! It was the undoing of Samson as it has undone many others. Keep us on guard against persons who substitute sex passion for love! Save us from those who would destroy perfect love. *Amen.*

May 3
REVENGE CREATES CONFUSION

"And the people came to Bethel." (Judges 21:2)

War had wrought havoc among the twelve tribes. The members of the tribe of Benjamin were slain with the exception of six hundred men who had escaped death and capture. There was a tradition that disaster would follow a time when the tribes were not intact. After thousands had been slain and they had come to the "house of God" in Bethel, it was found that no one responded from the tribe of Benjamin. A crisis had developed.

Meditation: Help us to know the value of the solidarity of the family. Bound to Jehovah through worship we are safe. When we sin help us to realize the enormity of the wrong and try to cover it with righteous acts for we know that You are forgiving! *Amen.*

May 4
REVENGE ALMOST LEADS TO EXTINCTION

"O Lord, . . . why has this come to pass in Israel, that there should be today one tribe lacking in Israel?" (Judges 21:3)

When they came to Bethel to worship, it was discovered that war on account of revenge had practically annihilated the tribe of Benjamin. The women had been slain and there was a vow among the tribes that none of them should give daughters as wives to members of the tribe of Benjamin. Worship had again made them aware that they were bound together by ties of love and devotion to Jehovah. Would the annihilation of the tribe of Benjamin ultimately be the annihilation of all Israel?

Meditation: May some of the tragic examples of history teach us that war, envy, revenge and sin of every kind leads toward extinction. Help us to eradicate the evils of destruction and foster the righteous ways of advance and growth. *Amen.*

May 5
DEVOTION TO GOD HELPS TO FIND A WAY

"And the people of Israel had compassion for Benjamin, their brother, and said one tribe is cut off from Israel this day." (Judges 21:6)

In the crisis it was devised that the men of Benjamin should be given safe passage to the feast that was held yearly at Shiloh. At the feast it was arranged that when the young women of the tribes were dancing, the Benjaminites, lying in ambush, should rush out and steal a wife among the girls of the tribe that had come to the feast to worship. A wife for each man. What a method of covering a wrong? What about the absence of morality in this sort of worship? Saul, named Paul of the New Testament came from the tribe of Benjamin. *Meditation:* May we have learned the enormity of revenge, jealousy, envy and war as a method of dealing with problems. Let us have peace by being peaceful. May we save nations by sharing and not by stealing! *Amen.*

May 6
HUMAN LOVE IS CONSTANT

"Elkanah . . . used to go up year by year from his city to worship although he loved Hannah he would give Hannah only one portion." (1 Samuel 1:1, 3, 4, 5a)

In spite of conflicts, revenge, treachery, wars, etc., human love continued. Polygamy was practiced. The home life was insecure. The family was not a unit. Captives were made slaves. Worship was regarded as essential by the minority. Elkanah, the husband of Hannah was worshipful and Hannah prayed for a child and told the priest, Eli, of her desire. Her prayer was answered and she became the mother of Samuel which means God hears or "heard of God." When still a child she dedicated him to God and when he was weaned she placed him in the care of Eli, the priest. In this period there is a remnant of righteous people. Who are the remnant people today?

Meditation: We are grateful that a remnant in Israel retained faith in You at a time when faithlessness was more popular than faithfulness. May we keep faith with Your faithfulness today and always! *Amen.*

May 7
THE ALL KNOWING GOD

"The Lord is a God of knowledge, and by him actions are weighed." (1 Samuel 2:3cd)

It is likely that this prayer of Hannah is the product of a relatively late editor. The poem shows a higher ethical content than the prose in which it is inserted. The folklore of the early Hebrews was repeated from one generation to another. Many of the poems and incidents have been lost but enough of them were preserved to give us a fair knowledge of the philosophy of the people.

Meditation: We believe, O God, that it is better to be with the remnant and to serve You than to be among the many and be disloyal. May we serve You at all times! *Amen.*

May 8
SAMUEL IS A FAITHFUL ADOLESCENT

"The boy Samuel continued to grow both in stature and in favor with the Lord and with men." (1 Samuel 2:26)

How this verse reminds us of the Lukan description of the youth of Jesus! (Luke 2:52) Hannah had dedicated Samuel to God. Eli, the priest, regarded him as priestly material. Eli was unfortunate in that his own sons were wicked and a disgrace to the priesthood. But the light of God had not been extinguished and Samuel became a medium to keep the lamp of redemption burning. Note the nature of the environment and early training of this youth. How important is it to begin training young people for Christian living and Christian work? What do you think of dedicated parents?

Meditation: We are thankful for the aspirations and visions of youth. To trust You will bring confidence and mission. May we teach our children the privileges and outreach of dedicated youth! *Amen.*

May 9

LET US LISTEN TO GOD

"It is the Lord; let him do what seems good to him." (1 Samuel 3:18c)

These are the words of advice by Eli to Samuel. God had already called his name several times but being young he did not respond. He, however, told Eli of his experience. Eli was familiar with the intimate communication from God and advised Samuel to respond to the voice and obey it. Both Samuel and Eli were submissive to the guidance of God and wanted God to work through them. Samuel became a famous leader and teacher in Israel. He is below the Christian standards in conduct but he was beyond the average person of his day in ability, insight and dedication. What do you think about young people making their own decisions?

Meditations: Help us to place ourselves in the care of God. May we contribute to the worthwhile efforts of mankind to supplant the cold war or any war with righteous and constructive service to God, our nation and ourselves! *Amen.*

May 10

SAMUEL IS DESTINED TO BE A PROPHET

"And all Israel from Dan to Beer-sheba knew that Samuel was established as a prophet of the Lord." (1 Samuel 3:20)

It was observed throughout Israel that Samuel was responsive and obedient to the God of Israel. He had a keen sense of ethics and of mission. Although the ethics of the time and the conduct of worship was less than Christian yet it was higher in content than that among the Philistines. Samuel must have taught and conducted worship in other places than Shiloh, in that he was known as a budding prophet by people from the North to the South. How much do you think Samuel had learned about the patriarchs, Moses and the leaders in the time of the Judges?

Meditation: Help us to foresee the possibilities of youth when they have a sense of mission. Help me to help young people to dedicate themselves to Christian living regardless of their vocation! *Amen.*

May 11
THE ARK IS CAPTURED

"The glory has departed from Israel! Because the ark of God has been captured." (1 Samuel 4:22b)

Things were bad in Israel. The Philistines were hostile. Eli was old. The people were disobedient and disconcerted. The ark, which symbolized the presence and power of God, was at Shiloh. As the battle between the Philistines and Israelites continued in the area near what is now Joppa, the Israelites were defeated and the ark was taken by the Philistines to Dagon. The sons of Eli were slain. Eli died and consternation in Israel followed. The ark is said to have contained "the testimony of the covenant, a pot of manna and Aaron's rod." In what sense had it protective value for the Israelites and destructive values for the Philistines? Did it hold a place among the Israelites similar to our flag?

Meditation: May God be present with us in spirit whether we have a symbol or not! May we continue to think of You as a Spirit unconfined? In any case give us a sense of Your presence to keep us steadfast! *Amen.*

May 12
PLACES OF WORSHIP AND JUDGMENT

"Samuel judged Israel all the days of his life. And he went on a circut year by year to Bethel, Gilgal, and Mizpah." (1 Samuel 7:15-16)

Samuel promoted the democratic way of living and judging. He was less a priest than a prophet. He urged the people to turn to God with their hearts and abolish false gods and symbols. Many obeyed. The religion of Israel was restored. In your reading about the ark of the covenant what was the greater force, the ark of the covenant itself or the ark as the symbol of the Presence of God? Samuel seems to have moved among the people and seems to have known God and understood people.

Meditation: O God, we believe that any symbol of Yourself makes You less than Yourself. We pray that nothing shall come between You and us. Help us to live as if You were always present to help us! *Amen.*

May 13
THE PEOPLE DEMAND A KING

"We will have a King over us." (1 Samuel 8:19c)

We have learned how the seeds of democracy were sown in the times of the patriarchs and Moses. Neighboring tribes had kings and the associations of the people with the pagan neighbors influenced them so that they demanded a king for themselves. Samuel advised against it but the clamor was great and Samuel had to cooperate in making Saul their king. Samuel was a seer and the people thought that he had unusual spiritual insight. People can err. It is interesting to observe that Saul was a member of the tribe of Benjamin which at one time was nearly annihilated.

Meditation: May we accept Your leadership, O God! May our democratic leaders prove to be more useful leaders than

most of the kings of Israel! Will You be our spiritual king?
Amen.

May 14
THE SPIRIT OF GOD COMES UPON SAUL

"The spirit of the Lord will come mightily upon you, and you shall prophesy." (1 Samuel 10:6a)

Samuel was gracious in introducing Saul although he opposed the idea of kingship. Saul at first seemed to be responsive to the leading of the spirit and joined a band of prophets, identified himself with them and made a splendid impression. Would that Saul had always worn the mantle of obedience to God and love for the people that the good man Samuel gave him! In a sense the demand for a political king was a backward step. It gave rise to the concept that Saul was a leader to whom they should be devoted rather than to the God of righteousness and love.

Meditation: Our Father, we know that particular issues in time change methods of action. If we ask for a king may it be for the kingship of Jesus! *Amen.*

May 15
DEMOCRACY PREVAILED

"Cursed be the man who eats food until it is evening and I am avenged on my enemies." (1 Samuel 14:24c)

The Philistines were strong. They fought against Saul and the people of Israel. Saul was inclined to be jealous and revengeful. In a time of desperation Saul vowed that anyone of his army who should stop to eat before evening and victory was won should be cursed. Saul's son, Jonathan, ignored the demand and ate some honey that he had scooped up with a rod. The penalty was death but the people intervened and would not let Saul carry out his vow. The claim of the people was that Jonathan had wrought a great victory to Israel. (1

Samuel 14:45) Jonathan recognized the authority of the king and would have submitted to be put to death if the people had not intervened. Can you trust the judgment of the people to do right?

Meditation: O God, may the people intervene now against every form of evil! May we have the courage to take proper measures to change a bad law. May we have just enough laws to keep us united for the general good! *Amen.*

May 16
THE REAL KING

"When the Lord your God was your King." (1 Samuel 12:12)

Both Gideon and Samuel seemed to think that God was King even when they themselves were influential leaders. They felt that they were acting for God and that the people were responsible to God rather than to them. This may have been a judgment of history concerning these two leaders. The seeds of democracy were certainly sown by Gideon and Samuel as they thought of themselves as agents of God. Do you think that Jesus may have read about these men and concluded that the real King is the one who heeds the voice of God. Is this the Holy Spirit helping man to understand God?

Meditation: We thank you, God, that the stream of democracy runs through much of the Old Testament and that any power less than God's power is wrong. May we always think of God as our King and ourselves as His agents! *Amen.*

May 17
KINDNESS IS REWARDED WITH KINDNESS

"You showed kindness to all the people of Israel when they came up out of Egypt." (1 Samuel 15:6b)

The Kenites, you remember, were the friends with whom

Moses lived when he was exiled from Egypt. Then Jethro, Moses' father-in-law, visited Moses in the wilderness and gave him advice and help. Now that the Israelites were warring against the Amalekites, with whom the Kenites must have been associated, Saul wanted to return this kindness and advised that the Kenites should depart so that in the battle against the Amalekites they would have no part. Saul showed kindness to the Kenites but hatred for the Amalekites. It is apparent that the philosophy of Saul was "like for like" rather than the way of Joseph. The Amalekites were defeated and the fact that Saul showed kindness manifests the fact that kindness in the long run makes for preservation, peace and salvation.

Meditation: Our Father, to favor those who favor us is normal but to favor those who dislike us is Christian. Help us to choose the Christian way because we are Christians! *Amen.*

May 18

SACRIFICE AGAINST OBEDIENCE

"To obey is better than sacrifice, and to hearken than the fat of rams." (1 Samuel 15:22)

This is part of an ancient poem that reflects changing ideas about God. Samuel seems to have interpreted that it was the will of God that Saul should destroy all the Amalekites and take their possessions. Saul had spared Agag, king of the Amalekites, and some of the animals. Samuel interpreted this as disobedience. Then Samuel himself hewed Agag to pieces at Gilgal. Was this an instance of the conflict of judgment? Both Saul and Samuel seem to have resorted to the law of revenge. However, through this instance we do have the statement that it is better to obey than to offer sacrifice. Does this add anything to our study of the substitution of man's revengeful acts with kindness and love?

Meditation: Teach us lessons, O God, through our experience.

Forgive Saul and Samuel for this backward step and help us to forgive and to be generous in interpreting Your will! *Amen.*

May 19
GOD LOOKS ON THE HEART

"Man looks on the outward appearance, but the Lord looks on the heart." (1 Samuel 16:7d)

The above statement of God to Samuel is a directive in keeping with God's concern and love. Under God's guidance David was anointed as a successor to Saul. The understanding of personality and the search for leadership is still the quest of man. We know that we should look deeper than on the outward appearance. We should rely more on mind and heart judgments than on appearance judgments. Was the character of David an advance over that of Saul? When we compare these men with Jesus we find that both fail to measure up to Christian standards of character. It required the coming of Jesus to show a consistent person who chose righteousness as his standard and love as his method.

Meditation: We thank You, Lord, for the truths that came from cloudy observations and experiences. May I search the minds of persons when I attempt to show judgment? *Amen.*

May 20
DAVID SHOWS STRENGTH

"I come to you in the name of the Lord of hosts." (1 Samuel 17:45c)

What a wonderful statement! David had not the stature of Goliath. He had no armor like Goliath. He did not want any. But he did have mental and spiritual armor that he gained as a shepherd lad who trusted in God. Is it true that each person has a Goliath to fight? If we have stones like those of faith, courage, knowledge, skill, devotion, trust and obedience we can overcome an enemy that at first glance seems invulnerable. We should always be on the side of God and never on the side of Goliath.

Meditation: May I have faith in God and skill to contend against my enemies. May I overcome an evil enemy with good. May I continue to hold that the armor of love, righteousness and peace is stronger than that of steel or iron! *Amen.*

May 21
LOVE YOUR NEIGHBOR AS YOURSELF

"Then Jonathan made a covenant with David, because he loved him as his own soul." (1 Samuel 18:3)

Jonathan, the son of Saul, and David became friends. They covenanted to befriend each other. That Jonathan loved David as he did himself is proved by his future loyalty. The devotion of these two important persons may have done much to originate and develop the second part of the great commandment, "You shall love Your neighbor as yourself." The story of the cooperation and trust that David and Jonathan had for each other is an outstanding historical example of its application. Read about David and Jonathan in your Bible.

Meditation: Seal our vows with Your Spirit, O God. May we learn that the strongest bond is that of love supported by Your love. We are grateful that the bond of friendship between Jonathan and David taught this truth! *Amen.*

May 22
THE SEAL OF THE COVENANT

"The Lord shall be between you and me." (1 Samuel 20:42b)

The covenant of Jonathan and David was sealed by the spirit of God's presence. When Saul became so jealous of David that he planned to kill him, David was befriended by Jonathan in a marvelous manner. Jonathan really endangered his own life and welfare in his friendship with David. Jonathan may have been among the first in history to have been willing to exemplify vicarious sacrifice. The covenant of these two men was never broken. Should we also think of God as the sealer of every marriage vow?

Meditation: When you guide us, our Father, we never have fear. May the seal of friendship that bound Jonathan and David bind each marriage vow and be the bond of every home! *Amen.*

May 23

JEALOUSY GENERATES EVIL

"Saul has slain his thousands, And David his ten thousands." (1 Samuel 21:11c)

This part of a very old song and party slogan has survived the test of time. The victories of David over the Philistines, the enemies of the Israelites, won praise from the people. The success of David in ridding Israel of the treacherous Philistines and the popular acclaim of the people angered Saul. He had failed to remember that it was David who killed Goliath in a crisis that made Saul's kingdom secure. The jealous nature of Saul caused him to become covetous. The allegiance of the people became divided and warring factions persisted. Should Saul have been happy at the success of David? How may jealousy divide a church or a nation? Does jealousy create weakness?

Meditation: May jealousy never weaken my faith or that of my friends! May I live humbly so that others will not become jealous! Help me to encourage others when they are succeeding in a good enterprise or mission! *Amen.*

May 24

THE LORD'S ANOINTED

"I will not put forth my hand against my lord: for he is the Lord's anointed." (1 Samuel 24:10d)

This portion of Scripture shows how David prayed for poise and mental strength in the face of opportunities to harm Saul. The dramatic act of David in proving his loyalty to Saul and the people when he had Saul at a disadvantage in Saul's own tent is historic. The inclusion of the ancient proverb "out of the wicked comes forth wickedness" seems to show that David thought Saul to be wicked and yet he was unwilling to avenge the wickedness of Saul by killing him. The cosmos and succeeding events through Saul's own misjudgments and mistakes became his avenger. (see 1 Samuel 24:13f)
Meditation: We praise You, O God, for the strength of David in a time of crisis and temptation. His loyalty to You did not conflict with his loyalty to a jealous king. Let us remember that wickedness destroys the wicked and that Saul according to history actually destroyed himself. *Amen.*

May 25

GOD IS THE FINAL JUDGE

"May the Lord judge between me and you, may the Lord avenge me upon you; but my hand shall not be against you." (1 Samuel 24:12)

David set a new pattern. He did not render "like for like" or show unlimited revenge. Saul was the anointed king and David in loyalty to Israel assigned the judgment of Saul to God. David evidently concluded that he himself was an agent of God to war against the Philistines but among his own people he believed that God was the final judge. David was a strict nationalist. His refusal to take vengeance on Saul set a new high in action. He regarded God as the avenger rather than himself. Did Jesus rely on the judgment of God rather than that of man? (John 18:28-40)

Meditation: It is heartening to know that Jesus went further in relying on the universality of the judgment and love of God. May we feel, O God, that the example of David gave Jesus an insight into the way of righteousness. We thank You for the teaching of history! *Amen.*

May 26

FRIENDSHIP IS INHERENT

"Saul said to David, You are more righteous than I; for you have repaid me good, whereas I have repaid you evil." (1 Samuel 24:17)

When Saul was humiliated before loyal David he had to admit in tears that David was more righteous than himself. To admit this truth must have been embarrassing to the king. His confession admits that to save is better than to kill and to withhold the sword is better than to avenge. Saul failed to repent and continued the feud. Would that this confession had canceled his jealous nature and had made him appreciative of kindness and loyalty. Future events must have proved to the people the power of forgiveness and loyalty in man aaginst the vengeance of man.

Meditation: When we confess our guilt, may we turn to righteousness and cover our wrongdoing with right doing! We believe that righteousness will lead into the abundant life, whereas revenge will ever haunt and plague us! *Amen.*

May 27

DAVID FORGIVES

"Blessed be the Lord who has avenged the insult I received at the hand of Nabal and has kept back his servant from evil: the Lord has returned the evil-doing of Nabal upon his own head." (1 Samuel 25:39)

When David was still an outlaw and freebooter, he protected Nabal's flocks and at sheep shearing time asked Nabal for a reward. Nabal gave an insolent answer that insulted David and his men. David was prevented from wreaking vengeance by the timely arrival of Abigail, Nabal's wife, with gifts and flattery. The next day Nabal informed about his stupidity had an apoplectic shock and died. David interpreted his death as the vengeance of God upon him. Later Abigail became one of the wives of David. Does this account of Nabal and David strengthen the idea that God is and should be the avenger and not man? Is it possible that the nature of the cosmos and moral law avenges wickedness? Is it because God is the creator and just that we can attribute vengeance to Him?

Meditation: Let the principle of righteousness teach us that the universe, itself, will take care of injustices. If God is just then the injustices to us will become just through the justice of God. *Amen.*

May 28

THE RIGHTEOUSNESS OF MAN

"The Lord rewards every man for his righteousness and his faithfulness." (1 Samuel 26:23)

As we read the surrounding verses in which this true statement is found we admire David for his loyalty and principles. He would not kill or injure the king when he had the opportunity but believed that God would reward the righteous and faithful. He did not attempt to avenge as most persons in his time would have done. He would not attempt to judge or avenge but left that to God. Through this episode Saul had to admit the integrity of David toward the people of the covenant. In time David became king through the natural course of events. Even Saul had to admit the moral superiority of

David and foresaw success for him. Was Saul a person who knew to do right but did it not?

Meditation: May I accept God's righteousness and His ability to be the ruling power at all times and places! *Amen.*

May 29
THE ULTIMATE OF WAR IS ANNIHILATION

"Abner called to Joab 'Shall the sword devour forever? Do you not know that the end will be bitter?'" (2 Samuel 2:26)

This is a crucial statement of truth. Abner was the general of the army of Ishbosheth, Saul's son. Joab and Abishai were the generals of David's army and both generals wanted to win in favor of his man. Who should be king? The two branches within Israel were at war and the battle was imminent. Abner knew that both sides would be weakened with the result that Israel itself would be weaker. This would make Israel a prey to a foreign power. Abner spoke first, Joab admitted the truth and the battle never started. The truth that war meant ultimate annihilation prevailed. David became king. How should we turn to peaceful means for peace in our time? Should we let the guns and battleships rust and turn our knowledge of atomic energy to useful and peaceful means?

Meditation: Our Father, it was learned long ago that wickedness is destructive and that love and kindness are saving values. Help us to obey this lesson from history and use our intelligence to save and to preserve mankind. *Amen.*

May 30
KINDNESS IS RECIPROCAL

"I will deal loyally with Hanum, the son of Nahash, as his father dealt loyally with me." (2 Samuel 10:2a)

The human mind tends to give kindness for kindness. There are persons, however, now as in the past who have so much cruelty and power in their minds that they fail to appreciate kindness. David was beyond this and showed kindness for kindness, especially among his own people. An interpretation of the Golden Rule means that if we like kindness and forgiveness for ourselves, we should show this spirit to others. The text suggests "like for like" rather than unlimited kindness. Is that true?

Meditation: Often, we pray that the minds of those who have been badly treated may regain faith in kindness. Inspire us with faith that defies despair and gives hope that will make the future more radiant. *Amen.*

May 31
NATHAN'S PARABLE

"He shall restore the lamb fourfold, because he did this thing, and because he had no pity." (2 Samuel 12:6)

David was not always consistent. He had no compunction about the treatment and killing of Philistines. For his own people he was inclined to be kind and forgiving. This clever parable by Nathan tells about the cruelty of a rich man over one who was poor. The rich man demanded the one ewe lamb of the poor man. As Nathan described the situation, the injustice of the rich man aggravated David. Then, at a timely moment, Nathan turned the parable on David, himself, in the use of his own power and position with Bath-sheba and the unjust treatment of her husband Uriah. Is it true that wrongdoing returns to plague us? Should human beings know how to treat each other in the spirit of the Golden Rule?

Meditation: As the parable shows the treachery and subtlety of sin so may we be strong that sin will not be committed. Knowing that sin will plague us, give us the will to resist sin and overcome it with good. *Amen.*

June 1

AN INTIMATION OF IMMORTALITY

"He is dead . . . I shall go to him, but he will not return to me." (2 Samuel 12:23)

The sin of David with Bath-sheba plaqued him. David prayed and did all that he could to save the child with Bath-sheba. The fact that the child did not live made David search for redemptive measures. He seemed to think that the vengeance of the universe was punishing him on account of his sin. This led him to think that although the child could not come to him he could go to the child. Is this an intimation of immortality? Is the idea of the eternal spirit beginning to take root in the minds of men like David?

Meditation: Life comes and goes whether we do or not. The universe seems to be created for survival. We cannot stop time. We set events in time. May we use time well and keep the events in time moral and within the line of righteous duty! *Amen.*

June 2

HUMAN LOVE AND HATRED

"The hatred with which he hated her was greater than the love with which he had loved her." (2 Samuel 13:15b)

This is a case where physical passion without divine love is weak. Illicit relations between the sexes created trouble and heartaches. Ammon had seduced Tamar. The sin was calamitous. Sin had turned the bodily urge into mental hatred with physical cruelty as a result. Irregular sexual relations create hatred and show weakness. Proper sexual relations foster real love and may become the medium through which parenthood is achieved. Parental love is a binding sacrificial love with both subjective and objective elements. Parental love is of God and has persisted through the centuries. Should the sense of doing right keep the mind in constant control over the body? Is it true that illicit physical relations produce hatred but that proper human relations binds the lovers into highest love? Which one of the Ten Commandments enjoins purity of the family?

Meditation: Help us to know and to keep proper social behavior in control. We ask this for individuals and society. May proper relations always exist in my family and in every family! *Amen.*

June 3
THE LAW OF BLOOD REVENGE PROVES WEAK

"Let the king invoke the Lord your God, that the avenger of blood slay no more, and my son be not destroyed." (2 Samuel 14:11)

Joab was disturbed because Absalom had been exiled. The family of David was estranged and divided. Joab devised a plan whereby a woman of Tekoa frantically proved to David the weakness and destructiveness of revenge within a family. When David expressed sympathy for the feigned plight of the woman it was suddenly shown to him how he had treated Absalom, his son. The "lex talionis" or law of "like for like" revenge proved weak and ineffectual.

Meditation: May the homes of our land be mediums to promote the general welfare. Help me to do nothing that will divide or destroy a home or a person! To know to do right should lead me to do right! *Amen.*

June 4
HOW DAVID TREATED AN ENEMY

"And David said . . . let him curse. It may be that the Lord will look upon my affliction, and that the Lord will repay me with good for this cursing of me today." (2 Samuel 16:11d, 12)

Shimei belonged to the group that favored Ishbosheth, Saul's son, to rule. When Absalom rebelled Shimei joined his forces. As David and his army marched through a valley Shimei cursed from the top of the hill and his men threw stones and dirt at David. Abishai, David's general in command, asked if he should send men to kill Shimei. David replied as above. The outcome was victory for David and this is an instance when David did not revenge a wrong. David again held to the principle that God would be the avenger. David proved to be right. Was the influence of David with forgiveness and kindness effective to guide future generations? *Meditation:* May faith grow with forgiveness! God guided David. The rebellion of Absalom failed. May our faith in doing right and showing kindness sustain us! *Amen.*

June 5

SHIMEI REPENTS

"The king said to Shimei, 'you shall not die.'" (2 Samuel 19:23)

David mourned for Absalom until Joab told him that the people resented his bereavement on the ground that he loved those who hated and rebelled against him and hated those who were loyal to him. This shows that David was disturbed at sin and wrongdoing in his own family. When David became secure as king, Shimei was among the first to apologize. David did not order that Shimei should be slain. Peace followed and David was again secure. Is revenge ever justifiable? *Meditation:* How can we further prove, O Lord, that it is right to be righteous and sinful to do wrong? May we have the courage to forgive and it may be that we shall be forgiven! *Amen.*

June 6
POETIC RESUME OF DAVID'S PHILOSOPHY
"Therefore, the Lord has recompensed me according to my righteousness, with the loyal thou dost show thyself loyal . . . With the pure thou dost show thyself pure . . . He is a shield, a rock, my strong refuge." (2 Samuel 22:25, 26-33)

This song of deliverance showed that David had learned basic principles the hard way. He had come to the conclusion that God is steadfast and will give justice by rewarding the righteous, showing mercy to the merciful and showing Himself to be a refuge. Sin is retroactive to the sinner. To do right makes God a refuge, a shield and a rock. Righteousness is also retroactive and if one is pure God becomes pure. If one is loyal God will be thought of as keeping the covenant.

Meditation: O God, we thank You that a study of David increases our faith in the nature of God. We learn that to do right makes right supreme and to do wrong produces guilt and guilt makes a disturbing conscience. *Amen.*

June 7

DAVID PRAISES GOD
"The Lord . . . has redeemed my soul out of every adversity." (1 Kings 1:29b)

As David's life was weakened on account of age he gave God credit for his success. Like a pendulum he swung back and forth while time passed on. In general, it may be said that he had a sense of compassion, respect for right, gave and accepted forgiveness and was a successful king. The idea that prevailed through the period of the Judges that only the strongest and cruelest could rule had lost its meaning. A new line of thinking began to prevail. How may we think of David as a pioneer?

Meditation: We thank You, God, for mental and spiritual insight. You have, through Your experience with mankind, given and inspired among men the Golden Rule and the Rule of Love, and we are grateful. May our choices be in keeping with Your righteousness! *Amen.*

June 8

SOLOMON'S REQUEST

"You have asked for yourself understanding to discern what is right." (1 Kings 3:11c)

Solomon succeeded David to the kingship. When he had disposed of possible or real enemies like Joab, Shimei, Adonijah and others he asked for understanding and this request may indicate his own feeling of insecurity in dealing with the pressing problems that followed the death of David. It would seem as we read about his reign that not all his choices were wise or within the scope of right understanding. His family life certainly was not exemplary. What is your idea of a Christian home? Wherein do you think that David failed? In what did he succeed?

Meditation: We pray for wisdom and understanding just as Solomon did. Without Your help we cannot solve properly the problems of the day. With Your help we may have the integrity of Joseph, the faith of Abraham and the insights of a prophet! *Amen.*

June 9

LOVE GUIDED THE DECISION

"Her heart yearned for her son . . . and she said to the king, 'Oh, my lord, give her the living child, and by no means slay it.' But the other said, 'It shall be neither mine nor yours, divide it.'" (1 Kings 3:26cd)

This case shows sacrificial love at its best. Parental love is sacrificial and life preserving. Two women claimed to be the mother of the same child and the case was brought to Solomon for judgment. After listening to the testimony Solomon called for a sword to divide the child. One woman pleaded for the life of the child while the other woman suggested that it should be divided and should then belong to neither. Solomon knew the power of parental love and decided that the woman who would preserve life was the real mother. Love gives itself. Love is subjective but is completed by the objects. Is the Love of God the object of our living? Could we have life without the plan of God's Love? Define Love!

Meditation: O God, we rejoice to learn that in primitive times the sacrificial nature of parental love was known. Help us to love You always! *Amen.*

June 10

GOD KEEPS HIS COVENANT

"O Lord God, there is no God like thee . . . keeping covenant and showing steadfast love to thy servants who walk before thee with all their heart." (1 Kings 8:23)

This prayer of Solomon may have had considerable influence in projecting the fact that God is Love and should be loved, and that He keeps His covenant with those who worship and live according to His will. The idea of love as a factor of God and man had been growing through the preceding centuries. The time had come when even a king proclaimed it. Meanwhile, the idea of man being his own avenger had been diminishing. The system of man as his own avenger had broken down. It seems to be implied in the above text that the unfaithful or covenant breaker creates his or her own problems. Have you ever broken a covenant? Have you ever made a bad vow?

Meditation: We thank You for the covenant relationship that we may have with You and with one another. To have a partner or partners in a great cause is heartening. May every cause in which man and God cooperate be a great cause! *Amen.*

June 11

GOD'S COMPASSION

"Forgive thy people who have sinned against thee . . . grant them compassion in the sight of those who carried them captive, that they may have compassion on them." (1 Kings 8:50ac)

This prayer attributed to Solomon assumes a condition of captivity that has passed. It reflects the compassion of God. Forgiveness to those in captivity and forgiveness to the captors by those in former captivity is one of the pathways of peace. Our study shows that God is becoming less a battle-god and more like a compassionate Father. Do you think that eras of peace with parental and marital love in homes has helped people to understand and accept the God of love?

Meditation: Glorify the present generation. Keep us faithful as we continue to build and dedicate temples, churches and buildings for Your worship. May we be consistent and dedicate ourselves to You! May each heart be made a temple! *Amen.*

June 12

THE DIVIDED KINGDOM

"Omri did what was evil in the sight of the Lord . . . he walked in all the ways of Jeroboam . . . and in the sins which he made Israel to sin." (1 Kings 16:25a, 26a)

The division of the kingdom after the death of Solomon and the introduction of pagan customs and gods hastened deterioration of the good conditions that had prevailed. Idolatry weakens. Sin and wrongdoing included misjudgments, bad ethics, wrong decisions, breaking of the covenant, loose living and the worship of other gods. Divisions always weaken the spirit of men and tend to make them lose faith in the power of God to lead and to heal. What about the strength of a divided church? Divided families create un-happiness. Can a divided kingdom stand?

Meditation: We know, our Father, that leadership is impor-tant. Weak leaders make a weak kingdom in the political field and weak leaders in a church make a weak church in the religious circles. Keep, we pray, the church united and if it is divided help us to unite it! *Amen.*

June 13

THE STILL SMALL VOICE

"And after the fire a still small voice." (1 Kings 19:12d)

In evil days with evil ways there may always be a remnant that hold to the covenant and try to make bad conditions better. The tendency of the Israelites to break the covenant and resort to the Baal religion divided the people, substituted pleasure without principle for religion and weakened sound judgments. Efforts were made to bring the people to their senses. Earthquakes, fires and other destructive forces came but the conditions did not improve. Finally the still small voice of God's Spirit was heard and accepted. A righteous remnant saved the nation.

Meditation: Our Father, was this still small voice a message of woe? Only after disaster and captivity had come would the people return to the simple ways of the desert when they were led and fed! *Amen.*

June 14

THE MINISTERING ANGELS

"An angel touched him, and said to him, Arise and eat." (1 Kings 19:5c)

Ahab, the king, was influenced by his wife Jezebel, a de-votee to Baalism, to use dramatic methods like exiling and killing the prophets of Israel. Elijah was one of the prophets who finally defied Ahab and Jezebel. Elijah had a hard time but he was cared for and sustained in remarkable if not miraculous ways. In the contest with the priests of Baal, Elijah was the champion. The Scripture shows how he was fed and comforted by angels and history records him as one of the greatest of contending prophets. Do we know when an angel comes to us? Do you think that an angel might be the better self or even another person who may give us spiritual food and insight when faith has nearly gone?

Meditation: In the midst of adversities give to us inner resources that will carry us through. Arouse me to acts of spiritual defense when evil assails me! *Amen.*

June 15
THE PROPHETS STAND FOR RIGHTEOUSNESS

"Elijah answered. I have found you, because you have sold yourself to do what is evil in the sight of the Lord." (1 Kings 21:20)

Ahab, supported by Jezebel, took possession of the vineyard of Naboth. For the unscrupulous method of taking the vineyard Elijah challenged them. He warned him about the vengeance of the universe and predicted bad days ahead, saying that at the very spot where Naboth was stoned, the blood of Jezebel should spill and be licked by the dogs of the street. Internal strife followed. Jezebel was thrown from a window in Jezreel and the dogs did lick her blood. The disasters that came to Ahab and Jezebel were real vengeance.

Meditation: We know that sin rebukes the sinner. May we never break the covenant as did Ahab and may we never be influenced by one who does not know the power of the God of love and compassion. May weak forms of worship never control me! *Amen.*

June 16
THE MANTLE OF ELIJAH IS PLACED
ON ELISHA

"Elisha said, 'I pray you, let me inherit a double share of your spirit.' " (2 Kings 2:9c)

Elijah and Elisha contended against the false religions, especially the Baal worship which was a fertility cult that in their worship sometimes resorted to lewd practices. Elisha asked for and received the mantle of Elijah. When he was carried by a whirlwind into heaven, Elisha said "My father, my father! the chariots of Israel and its horsemen!" (2 Kings 2:12) The ascension of Elijah supports the idea that God cares for his servants, and keeps the covenant by taking them to Himself. This is another intimation of immortality or the future life. Elijah and Elisha had power to heal. The words "My father, my father" show the intimacy of these prophets with one another and with God. Do you suppose Jesus read this and that it may have helped him to think and call God "Father?"

Meditation: Let the mantle of righteousness fall on me. Give me a double portion of Your righteous Spirit! Help me to overcome evil, first in myself, and then may I have power to help others! *Amen.*

June 17
THE BOOK OF THE LAW FOUND

"Hilkiah, the high priest, said, 'I have found the book of the law in the house of the Lord.' " (2 Kings 22:8a)

When Josiah was King the repairers and cleaners of the temple found the book of the law. It is apparent that interest in other areas for a generation or two had led to the neglect of the law and that even the book containing it was lost. Shaphan, the scribe, read it to the King. Huldah, the prophetess, pronounced it genuine. The book was read to the people and it was revealed that they had broken the covenant. The covenant was reaffirmed. The people revived the worship of God and the reign of Josiah gave them renewed faith and strength.

Meditation: If our ways are wrong, may some unique event turn us into the way that is right. May I correctly interpret the spiritual law of God! *Amen.*

June 18
GOD'S JUDGMENTS ARE UNIVERSAL

"He is the Lord our God; his judgments are in all the earth." (1 Chronicles 16:14)

The devotion to God or the lack of it brought advancement or retardation. The general tendency since Solomon had been downward. The wars with the Assyrians were weakening and fruitless. Many of the people had been deported to the Assyrian empire or killed. The books of Kings and Chronicles describe some of the highlights of disaster and also the revival periods as when Josiah was King and the book of the law was found and worship was restored. The philosophy in our text is a part of one of the poems or songs of appreciation for the remaining remnant that had kept the covenant.

Meditation: This text, O God, may reflect the teachings of Amos that You are God of all the people of the earth. We thank You that it is in keeping with Your creation, in that it is orderly, and You are merciful in Spirit! *Amen.*

June 19
GOD IS WITH THOSE WHO DO RIGHT

"Blessed be the Lord, the God of Israel, from everlasting to everlasting." (1 Chronicles 16:36a)

To this thanksgiving song of Asaph the people responded, "Amen." It is a beatitude that may have been used in temple worship or in the homes. The books of Chronicles retell the situations connected with the rise and fall of the tribes. The accepted philosophy is that God is good, His loving kindness is eternal and He has kept the covenant. Priests, prophets and people accept the compassion and goodness of God and there is much evidence that there were times when this definition of God was engraved on the foreheads as a constant reminder of eternity, control and love of God. What does the word blessed mean?

Meditation: If we obey God we will keep the laws already made and will make others that will support the ones we have. Obedience brings unity when one obeys the moral law that may be inherent and written on the heart! *Amen.*

June 20
ISRAEL IS JUDGED BY ISAIAH

"Your princes are rebels and companions of thieves. Every one loves a bribe . . . They do not defend the fatherless, and the widow's cause does not come to them." (Isaiah 1:23)

During the interim between the kingship of Solomon and the fall of Samaria in 722 B.C. many of the principles that had been learned in the wilderness and practiced in the time of David were ignored or forgotten. Isaiah lived in the midst of these times and could foresee dangers ahead. His insight has proved him to be one of the great prophets of all time. A prophet is one who has a philosophic insight with inherent principles that enables him to predict the future by the prevailing trends of the present. A prophet must know the righteousness of God. What is righteousness and what does it involve?

Meditation: May the judges of today be understanding and have philosophic insight. May they conform to standards that are in keeping with the Golden Rule! *Amen.*

June 21
THE COVENANT IS NOT KEPT

"Ah, Assyria, the rod of my anger, the staff of my fury."
(Isaiah 10:5)

God is personalized by the prophet. A nation like Assyria represents the anger of God at war with the Israelites. Could this anger of God be a Hebrew interpretation and expression that covered up the fact that they had broken the covenant, worshipped idols, neglected the widow and orphan and when they became weak they were an easy prey for the belligerent Assyrians? Can we think of God as disappointed and suffering because Israel had broken the covenant and done the things that the patriarchs taught should not be done?

Meditation: We are not here to dream, to shirk or drift
We have work to do, loads to lift!
Help me do what will bring You praise
Throughout the rest of my days. *Amen.*

June 22
THEY TRUST IN WRONG THINGS

"In returning and rest you shall be saved: In quietness and in trust shall be your strength." (Isaiah 30:15)

Isaiah taught that the above principles would help. The people were rebellious and had said "we will flee upon horses." They failed to realize that their pursuers would also be on swift horses. The same problem is with us today. Are we trusting in atomic missiles, rockets and hydrogen bombs too much? The leaders in Israel thought that they had superiority over their enemies, only to discover when it was too late that the enemy had superior equipment, skill and cleverness. In whom should the American people place their trust? Is the United Nations organization sufficient? Why not trust God and do right!

Meditation: Pride, we are taught, goes before a fall. Self-respect is better than pride. God does not like pride or precociousness. Will You keep us humble enough to trust in rightness above everything else! *Amen.*

June 23
FOREIGN HELP PROVES TO BE A SNARE

"Woe to those who go down to Egypt for help and rely on horses." (Isaiah 31:1)

One party advocated alliances with Egypt. The prophet in poetic terms advised against it. It tended to becloud the issue by placing faith in the prowess and strength of another nation rather than in God and in the efficiency of the people themselves. Isaiah's judgment proved to be sound. What about present day nations? Some think our reliance and alliance with Russia during World War II has proved to be disastrous. Are we placing too much faith in our military strength today? Is only trust in God and working in the ways of God sufficient to build strength and develop sound judgment for security?

Meditation: May each person who does wrong learn to do right through the penalty that caused suffering because of the wrong. May each person in our church and nation trust God and the voice of public opinion and conscience. *Amen.*

June 24
GOD IS TRUSTWORTHY

"The Lord is the everlasting God, the Creator of the ends of the earth. He does not faint or grow weary, his understanding is unsearchable." (Isaiah 40:28)

This concept of God should have induced the people to forsake the worship of idols and false notions about God. They were a nation old enough to know that this is God's world and He will take care of it. He needs the help and worship of all. If a person or nation is wicked, God through the cosmos He has created will use other people and nations to punish and avenge the wrongs of the people that are wicked. Noncooperation with God will delay the fruition of God's plan and curtail the freedom of man. God will not destroy what He has created. Man should in liberty work to help and to worship God and to live in peace.

Meditation: May each of us find the purpose and mission that will make us efficient for God and for ourselves. May the talent or talents we possess be multiplied by using them! *Amen.*

June 25

GOD WILL NOT FAIL US

"By his knowledge shall the righteous one, my servant, make many to be accounted righteous." (Isaiah 53:11bc)

This later prophet began to think of Israel as his servant and that suffering was due to the sins of others as well as the Israelites. There was suffering that was vicarious. Although conditions were bad, the prophet had faith in a remnant that would survive and in time teach Gentiles a way of salvation. Israel, as God's servant, had a mission. Those who kept the covenant would be saved, whereas those who broke the covenant would be separated. Have you ever failed God? Has God ever failed you? Can we say that man and nature may make mistakes?

Meditation: We are grateful for what the people of Israel brought and taught us. From their experiences and searchings we have inherited the knowledge of righteousness. *Amen.*

June 26

GOD'S FAVORITE PEOPLE

"You only have I known of all the families of the earth; therefore I will punish you for all your iniquities." (Amos 3:2)

Other people had transgressed and had their own troubles but Israel had special care because they were a covenant people. It was, however, the duty of Israel to respond and to obey in order to avoid punishment as chastisement. Israel and God must walk together and nature itself teaches that a common bond is necessary for progress and security. Because of God's concern for Israel the people had a deeper responsibility to keep the covenant and to walk with God. This was the primary message of Amos.

Meditation: How often, O God, have we failed as individuals. We have had the blessings of peace a long time and we have defiled one another. We have been given a work to do but we have not done it well. Forgive us and redeem us, and may our future deeds be worthy of the redeemed! *Amen.*

June 27

THE DAY OF THE LORD

"Woe to you who desire the day of the Lord!" (Amos 5:18a)

A party in Israel took comfort in wishing for the day of the Lord. The members of this party seemed to think that there would be a time when Israel would be favored and other people punished. Amos taught that God had no favorites. Obedience to Him was the requisite of all in order to survive. The continued delays, disappointments, casual worship, the neglect of the widow and orphan, etc. militated against Israel so that the day of the Lord would be one of war and destruction instead of good. Israel had privileges and favors to be sure, but these should impel the people to do right and to keep the covenant. They, however, should remember that other people and nations were also His people and a part of His creatorship. Did Amos preach the universality of God? Was this a new idea?

Meditation: Let us make this the day of the Lord! He has given it for our use and enjoyment. May God work through us to have other people believe that each day should be the day of the Lord. *Amen.*

June 28

GOD'S MESSAGE IS ONE OF JUSTICE

"Let justice roll down like waters, and righteousness like an ever flowing stream." (Amos 5:24)
"Seek good and not evil that you may live." (Amos 5:14)
"Hate evil, and love good, and establish justice in the gate." (Amos 5:15)

Amos gave these principles. They should prevail because God is a God of justice. We should be just and any disobedience will bring punishment and it might mean annihilation. The conduct of the people made Amos think that the time of reckoning was near. He warned them to turn to God, repent, seek good and hate evil. A time for judgment was inevitable. When is a day of judgment?

Meditation: May we turn to the way of righteousness and seek forgiveness while there is time. If we have the love of Yourself in our hearts we believe that we will be just, and if we are seeking to be just then we may have the guidance of a just God. *Amen.*

June 29

THE PROPHET OF LOVE

"You are 'sons of the living God.'" (Hosea 1:10 A.V.)
"I will have mercy upon her." (Hosea 2:23 A.V.)

Hosea had an unfortunate experience. It gave him a clue to the nature of God. His wife proved unfaithful and went after false lovers who made extravagant promises. She finally became destitute and was sold on the slave market. Hosea still loved her, bought her back and forgave her. She became a mother to their children. Hosea through this experience interpreted that Israel had sinned and gone after other gods. God, however, would forgive if the people would repent and turn to God. Israel should have learned the lesson that evil separates and destroys. To Hosea the mercy of God was immeasurable. Because of Hosea's faithfulness in a bad situation he learned that God is faithful and keeps the covenant.

Meditation: We are thankful for the warnings that are constantly being given about results when parents fail to love and care for their children, and when children fail to respond to their parents, or when alcohol is used in excess and when communism prevails. *Amen.*

June 30
THE COVENANT IS LIKE A MARRIAGE

"I will betroth you to me forever; I will betroth you to me in righteousness and in justice, in steadfast love, and in mercy. I will betroth you to me in faithfulness; and you shall know the Lord." (Hosea 2:19-20 A.V.)

This is part of an ancient Jewish marriage ceremony. The idea of Hosea was that the ceremony that bound him to Gomer was similar to the covenant that bound Israel to Jehovah. Because the people had not kept their part of the covenant they had sinned—committed whoredom—been unfaithful. The love of Hosea for Gomer was so genuine and his pledge so binding that he could forgive. In like manner, he claimed that God would forgive and take back the people if they would repent and return to Him.

Meditation: Let parental, marital and filial love prevail. They help to teach the deep love of God. Keep me faithful to my marriage vow! *Amen.*

July 1

GOD REFLECTS

"When Israel was a child, I loved him . . . I taught Ephraim to walk, I took them in my arms . . . I led them with cords of compassion, with the bands of love, and I became to them as one who eases the yoke on their jaws, and I bent down to them and fed them." (Hosea (11:1a, 3, 4)

Hosea presents a reflective God Who had taught and befriended His people. Yet they were ungrateful and were worshipping other gods that were imposters and deceivers. How severe should be their chastisement? Should a child always be faithful to a parent? Since God had done so much for Israel, why did not the people respond and love Him as He had loved them? How should parents deal with an ungrateful child? Are there people unworthy of parenthood?

Meditation: God is right and right will win. To doubt is disloyalty and to falter is a sin. Through parental and marital love You taught Hosea the closeness of Thyself. We are Your children and You have a right to expect obedience. Should one become prodigal let him or her return as did Gomer! *Amen.*

July 2

ISRAEL WILL NOT BE COMPLETELY DESTROYED

"I will not again destroy Ephraim; for I am God and not man." (Hosea 11:9b)

"My heart recoils within me, my compassion grows warm and tender." (Hosea 11:8ef)

On account of unfaithfulness the kingdom had already been divided into Israel and Judah. Division led to weakness as it always does. Must Israel accept an Assyrian King? Although the people will become afraid and tremble as a dove, yet a remnant will remain faithful so that the houses will be restored and the worship of God resumed. Hosea felt that the

people had erred in turning to false gods, but he believed that
God would forgive for He is a God of compassion.

Meditation: Have mercy upon us as You had mercy upon
Israel in the time of their deflection. May we worship God,
our Saviour, and build morality, social justice, economic freedom, economic righteousness and patriotic loyalty. Keep us
self-reliant and self-respecting! *Amen.*

July 3

GOD WILL HAVE COMPASSION

*"I am the Lord your God from the land of Egypt; you know
no God but me, and besides me there is no saviour."* (Hosea
13:4)

Hosea thought that God's love and compassion was the
deepest attribute of His nature. Although He was compassionate, the sins of Israel and Judah gave Him distress. Israel had
broken the covenant but He would forgive. How could He
give up the people who had once known Him? Hosea is often
called the "Herald of God's love." Should we, at this time,
make the love of God so supreme that our faith and actions
will be consistently Godlike?

Meditation: May our love be as deep as Yours, as patient
and as forgiving as Yourself. May we be pained for wrongdoing so that we will turn from evil and do good. May I
never let anything or anyone separate You from myself!
Amen.

July 4

GOD WILL HAVE MERCY

*"In thee the orphan finds mercy. I will heal their faithlessness;
I will love them freely."* (Hosea 14:3c, 4ab)

Hosea was pained on account of the sins of the people and
he believed that God was pained within Himself. Like Amos
and other prophets he was convinced that the fault of Israel

was that the people had not kept the covenant and were unfaithful. God, however, was merciful and would heal their
backslidings, help them to return to their own land and give
them back their houses if they would only return to God
and work righteousness. Do you think these words of Hosea
were spoken during or after the war with Assyria?

Meditation: You, O God, will heal our backsliding. You will
forgive our sins and we may continue to be free in thought,
word and deed. We repent of our sins and know that the
freest people are those who find it through Yourself! *Amen.*

July 5

GOD WAS HOSEA'S IDEAL

*"Sow for yourselves righteousness, reap the fruit of steadfast
love."* (Hosea 10:12ab)

The word description that Hosea gives of God's love is
superb. He taught Israel to walk, led him out of Egypt,
carried him in his arms, placed him where he could rest and
gave him food and shelter. The compassions of God never
ceased. He, therefore, would not completely destroy. Israel
suffered not by the will of God but by their own sins of rejection. Punishment lies within the universe itself, for the sake
of discipline, and God does not change it. He will redeem if
they would only turn to Him. They needed to sow righteousness to reap the fruits of love. What is a backslider? Are
people rejecting the way of God today? Do you have any
nations in mind that you think are rejecting God? Do you
think Jesus had read the book of Hosea?

Meditation: May we accept discipline. May the sense of guilt
prevent me from doing further wrong acts that will increase
my guilt! Let no obsession separate me from You! *Amen.*

July 6

MICAH'S CONCERN

"O my people, what have I done to you? In what have I wearied you? Answer me." (Micah 6:3)

Hosea's concept of God was that of a family relationship wherein a covenant had been made. Micah was disturbed because the people were ungrateful. They had the idea that they were the chosen people of God and that no harm would come to them regardless of their disloyalty and conduct. They had a false faith. Micah was certain that this idea of God was not in keeping with His goodness and mercy. The prevailing concept in social life was to "hate the good and love the evil" Micah 3:1-2, and this to Micah was a wrong philosophy concerning a patient, compassionate God of all the people of the earth.

Meditation: May we never become so proud or have seeming self-sufficiency that we will make evil good and good evil! Let each of us have a living conscience as living persons should! *Amen.*

July 7

DO YOU REMEMBER?

"O my people . . . remember . . . that you may know the saving acts of the Lord." (Micah 6:5ad)

Memory is one of the gifts of the spirit to man. It is a function of the mind that helps to keep us steadfast. Micah, like Hosea, wanted the people to remember the history of God in His dealings with the Israelites. He had led them from slavery to freedom and given them leaders like Moses, etc. They were able to resist the attacks of enemies. There were men like Balak who would destroy Israel but there were also men like Balaam that remained loyal to Israel and would only work and prophesy good. If they would remember what God had done they would cease to do evil and would work only what was good and keep the tradition of the people of Abraham. What are some of the traditions of the American way of life? How do you think we can undergird our nation with God?

Meditation: Let us remember what our fathers did to have liberty and to secure it for us. Let us read the Declaration of Independence, the compact of the Pilgrims and the Constitution of the United States to learn what freedom means. *Amen.*

July 8

WHAT GOD REQUIRES

"He has showed you, O man what is good." (Micah 6:8a)

Micah was convinced that man knew what he ought to do. Burnt offerings were of no value. Idolatory was not pleasing. Unfaithfulness to the covenant and disobedience in any of the commandments was wrong. Deceitful weights and balances were abominable. Perversion of justice was evil. Wickedness had many times been proved destructive. Man had learned what was good and, therefore, no blame should be attached to God. Does man always know what is best?

Meditation: Through history and our own experiences we have learned to know the power of righteousness to build and of unrighteousness to destroy. May each of us be alert, prayerful and obedient to the way we call right! *Amen.*

July 9

POSITIVE REQUIREMENTS

"What does the Lord require of you but to do justice, and to love kindness, and to walk humbly with your God." (Micah 6:8)

Religion furnishes a dynamic for ethics. An inner conviction determines the duty of one toward another. Justice, kindness, love, humility are primary elements of the Jewish,

Moslem and Christian religions. Duty toward man is made synonymous with duty toward God. One must know how to receive and to give justice, kindness and to exemplify humility. Micah prepares the way for the union of the two great commandments which Jesus cited as fulfilling the embodiment of the law and the prophets. Can one love his neighbor as himself? What do we mean by self-love? Can it be a blessing to a person?

Meditation: We thank You that Micah's definition of religion has been preserved for us. It has stood the test of centuries. It was surpassed only when Jesus with his genius combined the two GREAT COMMANDMENTS. Help us to keep Micah's definition. *Amen.*

July 10

GOD IS GRACIOUS

"The Lord, a God merciful and gracious, slow to anger and abounding in steadfast love and faithfulness." (Exodus 34:6b)

We turn to the book of Exodus because we believe that this concept of God, developed through experience and proclaimed by the prophets, became the analysis of God that grew out of much tribulation and searching. God is no longer an angry God but one who is near, answers prayers and speaks to his children, the prophets, in a language that they can understand. His creative way automatically punishes the wicked, rewards the righteous and supports the just. Obedience encouraged success and disobedience brought forth trouble. Do we agree that God is approachable, gracious and faithful?

Meditation: May the teachings of the prophets be our teachings now. We thank You that we can place Jesus among the prophets. Keep us steadfast in faith with righteousness! *Amen.*

July 11

GOD'S SOVEREIGNTY

"I will be gracious to whom I will be gracious, and will show mercy on whom I will show mercy." (Exodus 33:19cd)

God is both Creator and Sovereign. It is man's duty and within his ability to obey God. It is futile for man to try to be as God. It is just as foolish for a man to think that he can get along without God. God's laws are fixed for our general welfare. It is the duty of the individual to work in harmony with God's will and then God's graciousness will be apparent. He is gracious and has given man liberty. Man cannot make evil good but he can overcome evil with good. God is committed to the principles of righteousness and mercy. Man cannot change the laws of God, but God can, although He seldom does. There is nothing impossible with God. Man may delay the purpose of God but he cannot change it. What does God want me to be and do? What are the nature of the laws of God?

Meditation: May we accept the laws of the universe and assume that God has given them for our good! *Amen.*

July 12

THE PERIOD OF REFORM

"Forgive, O Lord, thy people Israel, whom thou hast redeemed." (Deuteronomy 21:8a)

This statement may be a reflection of the reform under King Josiah. It is far-reaching. Instead of being revengeful, it was better to mitigate the ancient law of revenge and wash one's hands in the blood of a sacrificed heifer. (Deuteronomy 21:1-9) This formula, with a prayer for forgiveness, tended to cover up the guilt of murder when the murderer was unknown. This reflects a period when blood revenge was justified but limited only to the known person who had committed the deed. It is a sort of compromise to the ancient law of revenge.

Meditation: Forgive the wrongs we may do to others. Let us cover our sins with righteous acts that we ourselves may do. May we turn the other cheek, do good for evil and do our part to think of revenge as a practice of primitive and not of cultured people! *Amen.*

July 13

GOD IS FAITHFUL

"Hear, Q Israel: The Lord our God is one LORD: and you shall love the Lord your God with all your heart, and with all your soul and with all your might." (Deuteronomy 6:4-5)

We have learned that Moses taught God's care and concern for his people. We know that Micah preached that religion consisted of justice, kindness and mercy with humility. It is in the book of Deuteronomy (second law) where God reveals Himself as One to be loved for Himself alone. His goodness and love merits loyalty, obedience and love. The repetition of the Shema by every loyal Jew each day has had a practical value in emphasizing that God is love and not vengeful. The idea of one God may have been late in developing. It came into being when the concern and care of God for His people surpassed that of any of the other known gods of the neighbors so that they came to the conclusion that there was only ONE GOD and He was superior to all other notions of a Supreme Being. Are you interested in searching for the development?

Meditation: We rejoice that the people came to think of God as worthy of love for the sake of His love. His demands are not grievous although they are exacting. Help us to accept exactness! *Amen.*

July 14
GOD LOVED THE PATRIARCHS FOR THEMSELVES
"The Lord set his heart in love upon your fathers." (Deuteronomy 10:15a)

God loved the fathers for themselves. Abraham was daring, adventurous and compassionate. Jacob was persistent. Joseph did right in the face of severe temptations. Jacob prayed for forgiveness and reconciliation and received both from God and his brother Esau. Isaac remained loyal to the practices of Abraham. The brothers of Joseph were repentant. Joseph became a saviour to his brothers and father. God was and should be loved for Himself.

Meditation: May the teachings and examples of our fathers stir us into action so that our devotion to freedom and to God may avail much. May we undergird our liberties with the Spirit of Jesus who said "I am the Bread of Life." (John 6:35) *Amen.*

July 15
GOD'S PATIENCE

"He will renew you in his love." (Zephaniah 3:17d)

In the time of Zephaniah, wars, exile and captivity had taken a great toll and to him the only hope that remained was in the saving of a remnant. The hope of a continuing great earthly kingdom had to be abandoned. He thought that this remnant would be pure, devoted and reliable. He evidently felt that the wicked were gradually being eliminated. Those who would survive were loyal and devoted to the service of the God of their fathers. He may have felt that those returning from captivity would have learned lessons that would help them morally and structurally. Zephaniah had faith in God's love and its power to help the faithful.

Meditation: Your patience, O God, is immeasurable. Your love for people does not weaken or disappear. You have created us for Yourself and we have justification for being restless until we abide in You. *Amen.*

July 16

GOD HIMSELF IS A REFUGE

"He knows those who take refuge in Him." (Nahum 1:7c)

The word Nahum means comfort. God's goodness and care for us should be inherent. The people may reject Him and worship other gods but this will bring only frustration and guilt. God will still be in control and His compassion will be continuous to those who honor and obey Him. God is a comfort in time of trouble. This may have been the period when Psalms like the forty-sixth (God is my refuge and strength— Psalm 46:1a) were written. Having lost faith in the help of pagan nations, only God was a source of help. Does God use nations to discipline other nations?

Meditation: You are the same yesterday, today and forever. Your might, willingness and ability to help is immeasurable. Help us to live to help ourselves. *Amen.*

July 17

GOD IS FAITHFUL

"The righteous shall live by his faith." (Habakuk 2:4b)

Although Ninevah and other cities may fail, yet God will continue his righteousness. Faith will support the righteous and a remnant will survive. It was felt that faithfulness to God and loyalty to the covenant were sources of strength for survival. The fact that the prophets were able to distinguish righteous living by their faith or their faithfulness the fact remains that the righteous have a high chance for survival. Do you believe that being faithful to God is a source of strength?

What does faithfulness to God embody?

Meditation: Let Your strength support my own, Your will my will and Your love my love. Inspire me to keep my mind and heart fixed in faith and faithfulness. *Amen.*

July 18
THE PHILOSOPHY OF JEREMIAH

"Shall I not punish for these things? says the Lord, and shall I not avenge myself on a nation such as this?" (Jeremiah 9:9)

This verse in Jeremiah describes a deceitful people. The hearts of the people were not with God. Jeremiah's own life was threatened. (Jeremiah 26:8-15) A question in the mind of this prophet was whether the whole nation would be destroyed. Would the righteous be destroyed with the wicked? He tried to reason; he thought that man was as intelligent as the migratory birds. The people were not all bad and some would return to God. He concluded that a remnant would survive. The whole nation, he thought, would not be destroyed.

Meditation: May we have faith in the survival not only of the remnant but of the whole nation. Whether we reject the universe or not we must deal with it and whether we accept God as friendly or not we must reckon with a consistent and living God. *Amen.*

July 19
THE GUIDE OF YOUTH

"Have you not just now called to me, 'My father, thou art the friend of my youth.'" (Jeremiah 3:4)

Jeremiah felt that the sins of Judah had been written with an indelible pen, but he could not think that the sins would cancel all the goodness and achievements. Judah was still a nation. A symbol that helped Jeremiah was a girdle. As a girdle clings to and surrounds the body so God still clings to the whole house of Israel and Judah. Judah had called "my father" and had not turned from God. Surely, Jeremiah thought, the people will learn to do right and to keep the covenant since they have seen what happened to disloyal and unfaithful Israel. Do you think the prophets learned much when they read about the experiences of the patriarchs?

Meditation: As the vine clings to the tree so may I cling to You. May I have a measure of satisfaction when I receive Your spirit. Having a life to live, let me live it for You! *Amen.*

July 20
THE SOURCE OF COMPASSION

"My anguish, my anguish! I writhe in pain! Oh, the walls of my heart!" (Jeremiah 4:19)

The authorized version translates the first two words "my bowels, my bowels," and that may be more correct. The prophet was pained within on account of the sins and impending destruction and captivity. It suggests the bowels and heart as the seat of compassion. When wrong is done pain and distress follows. At a time of crisis or great stress the "intestines and heart" seem to ache. Jeremiah ached. The sins of Judah had created stress. Physicians today claim that worry, stress, etc. cause ulcers. When embarrassed the blood pressure may rise. Have you been worried so that you were inwardly pained? Jeremiah really knew the location of pain. Because of the rejection of the covenant it worried the prophet.

Meditation: Let us live and act so that distress may be kept at a minimum! Let us do what will give ease to the conscience and peace to the mind. The organs of the body are bound with nerve cords. We are bound to You! *Amen.*

July 21

THE NEW COVENANT IDEA

"Behold, the days are coming, says the Lord, when I will make a new covenant with the house of Israel and with the house of Judah." (Jeremiah 31:31)

The Northern kingdom had been overthrown by the Assyrian army. Judah was weak. Some thought that a similar fate was near. The popular explanation of the fall of Samaria was the breaking of the covenant by the people. The interpretation of the covenant by the people may have been faulty in that the popular belief was that God would take care of the people of Israel regardless of their conduct or worship. Jeremiah could see no help for the people of Judah for they had the same interpretation. The stress of Jeremiah on account of the sin and wrong concept left no hope for salvation. Being pained in his own heart he originated or presented for the first time the idea of a new spiritual covenant.

Meditation: May we obey Your will and be saved for we know that if we disobey You and alienate ourselves from You we are lost. May we live with You through our righteousness! *Amen.*

July 22

THE NEW COVENANT DESCRIBED

"I will put my law within them, and I will write it upon their hearts." (Jeremiah 31:33b)

The former covenant was regarded as a legal covenant and seemed to carry with it the idea that it was God's handiwork. Therefore, He would care for Israel. Being descendants of the patriarchs, they felt they were a privileged people. The fall of Samaria showed they were not. Jeremiah conceived the idea of a spiritual covenant in the heart. To reject or to disobey God would bring discomfort. Rejection of God today often causes guilt which in turn creates discomfort and illness. What do we mean philosophically by the SELF?

Meditation: We are Yours and we know You will befriend us on condition that we are friends of Yours and try to do Your will. Consecrate me now to Your service, Lord, by the power of grace divine! *Amen.*

July 23

WE ARE GOD'S PEOPLE

"I will be their God, and they shall be my people." (Jeremiah 31:33c)

This places the relationship of God upon the people themselves instead of the priesthood. There need be no intermediaries. It is written on the hearts. The new covenant is spiritual and realistic just as the love of God is man and man's love to God. If a person does God's will his best SELF will praise him. If he does wrong his best SELF will scold him. Wrongdoing creates estrangement and frustration unless the doer of wrong repents and turns to God for forgiveness. Do you think there is need of an intermediary like a saint or priest for you to approach or talk with God?

Meditation: We are grateful that we may be Your people in our own right! Help us to sense that You are nearer to us than breathing. As we do not want to lose a member of the body so we do not want to lose You! *Amen.*

July 24

THE PEOPLE KNOW GOD

"For they shall all know me from the least of them unto the greatest of them." (Jeremiah 31:34b)

To know God is a constant quest of man. God knows us because He breathed Himself into us. The future need is to know God as Spirit so that the spirit of man may coordinate with the Spirit of God. God is approachable for each person.

They may all know Him and have no need of a priest, saint, cloud, fire or tabernacle and yet all of these may be a help in knowing God.

Meditation: Jeremiah found You to be as intimate with him as he was with his own self. The SELF is what we are. Sometimes we are confused about our own real SELF. To know YOU will help us to know ourselves! *Amen.*

July 25

GOD WILL FORGIVE

"For I will forgive their iniquity, and I will remember their sin no more." (Jeremiah 31:34d)

Forgiveness is a factor in the new spiritual covenant relationship. Forgiveness will be complete so that the remembrance of the past unfaithfulness will be blotted out. God will freely take back those who return. The new covenant is the basis of Jesus' own teaching. It was appropriated by Jesus at the Last Supper and supplied the basis of the New Testament doctrine of salvation. (Hebrews 10:14-18) The new covenant is the top stone of Jeremiah's spiritual edifice. It seems to be the top stone of Jesus' teaching also. It is in keeping with Jesus' statement "God is a Spirit." (John 4:24a)

Meditation: Make each of us a member of the spiritual covenant! When we make promises may they be written on the heart as well as upon a document! *Amen.*

July 26

EACH PERSON IS RESPONSIBLE

"Everyone shall die for his own sin; each man who eats sour grapes, his teeth shall be set on edge." (Jeremiah 31:30)

The old or legal covenant was made with Abraham and should have been binding upon his descendants. The new covenant was made with the people and was binding upon all people. This means that each person was responsible for his own acts. Both Ezekiel and Jeremiah held that the proverb "the fathers have eaten sour grapes, and the children's teeth are set on edge" was outmoded. Through the new covenant we are not responsible for the sins of our fathers but we are responsible for our own sins. If we eat sour grapes we must not blame another for the discomfort. What right have we to blame others for our own sins, our mistakes, our accidents? *Meditation:* Being a person let me act as a person should! May I not blame others for my own wrongdoing. Give me knowledge and let me have moral insight to use that knowledge well! *Amen.*

July 27

RETURN TO GOD

"Return, faithless Israel, says the Lord, I will not look on you in anger, for I am merciful." (Jeremiah 3:12)

The centralized cult had proved ineffective. They did not keep the covenant but repeatedly slid back into former evil ways and worship. They were urged to return. Jeremiah hoped that the people would return and obey the covenant, but later he decided that this hope would not be fulfilled. He looked forward to the making of the new covenant. Both Jeremiah and Habakuk thought that salvation to the nation would come through faithfulness. They must be on the side of God and not expect God to be on their side. God cannot be on the side of evil. He is merciful and righteous. What is mercy?

Meditation: Help us to return to You if we find that our faith is becoming weak. Complacency as a habit is dangerous. Keep us active doing Your work! *Amen.*

July 28
THE PROPHET OF THE EXILE

"He shall surely live; he shall not die." (Ezekiel 18:21b)

Ezekiel was a faithful pastor to the captives that were taken to Babylon. He attributed their plight to evil. They had profaned God's Holy name. The punishment, he thought, was due them. They had called for it. Ezekiel held that all souls belonged to God and that each should pass under the rod of judgment. Each person was responsible for himself and his own acts. Each person could be forgiven. Persons would live or die according to the trust and faithfulness they had in God. God is faithful and will redeem the repentant.

Meditation: Give us strength to stand upon our own feet both physically and morally; we are thankful that each of us is accounted responsible for his own conduct! *Amen.*

July 29

A NEW HEART AND A NEW SPIRIT

"Cast away from you all the transgressions . . . and get yourselves a new heart and a new spirit." (Ezekiel 18:31)

The time had come when the hope of Ezekiel was in a new covenant. If the remnant had this new covenant in each heart and spirit then Judah would be redeemed. This new heart and spirit would constitute a moral force within them. It had to be the spirit of God at work in their minds. This spirit would keep them obedient to God and idol worship would be abandoned. Is this new heart and spirit the ruling passion of the members of Israel in Palestine today? Will the present survival of Israel depend on the fact that they possess the land or upon the moral integrity that they exemplify through the years ahead?

Meditation: Give us a clean heart, for we are told that the pure in heart are blessed. If a new heart is needed let it be pliable, forgiving, generous and loyal to the God of Righteousness! *Amen.*

July 30

THE HOLINESS CODE

"You shall not hate your brother in your heart, but you shall reason with your neighbor, lest you bear sin because of him." (Leviticus 19:17)

There are several law codes in the book of Leviticus. Ezekiel may have had a part in developing a new set of rules to guide the spiritual life of the people. The new covenant had no place for vengeance or hatred. Hatred is the opposite of love and when one loves, hatred is absent. Love at its best cancels hatred. The remnant with the new code offered a new beginning. This change of thought developed from the sad experience of the exile in Babylon.

Meditation: We are thankful for the splendid rules of the holiness code. It shows transition from cruder codes of the past. Let Your spirit be in us so that each of us may be in tune with Your spirit! *Amen.*

July 31

VENGEANCE IS NOT IN MAN'S AREA

"You shall not take vengeance or bear any grudge against the sons of your own people." (Leviticus 19:18a)

The Holiness code obliterates vengeance as a way to have justice or to "get even," or to be nasty or mean. Former experiences with man being an avenger tended toward the weakening of Israel. Vengeance it may be said did not work. The chain reaction was vicious. Revenge among men was working against God and God was love. Efforts to lessen the harshness of revenge failed. God was love and cared for people and love did not work with revenge among men. Was

Judah among the first nation or people to question the law of vengeance?

Meditation: Give us hearts of compassion. Take away any spirit of revenge or retaliation. False pride by setting oneself as a revenger makes oneself a poor judge. *Amen.*

August 1
THE IMPORTANCE OF THE SELF

"You shall love your neighbor as yourself." (Leviticus 19:18b)

The ending of this text with the words "I am the Lord" defines the source of this conclusion. The standard of judgment is positive. It is individual in character. A person here is asked to place himself or herself in the place of the person as an object, and then act in accordance with his own self-respect, self-standards, self-love and self-judgment. It assumes that the subject or person has intelligence and can make intelligent judgment before each act. The standard for judgment is the way of LOVE. The SELF is raised to a high degree in importance. It is assumed that the other person as object has intelligence. What is the SELF and what is self-love?

Meditation: We are grateful for life and love in each person. Both are your gifts and we want to hold on to them. The fact that we never complete life or love and that we want to live longer and do more for those whom we love is strong evidence of the need for immortality. It requires the future life to complete this life on earth. *Amen.*

August 2
LAMENTATIONS

"His compassions fail not." (Lamentations 3:22 A.V.)

The author relies on the mercies of God. His compassion was evident in the preservation of the remnant. (Lamentations 5:1-6) The transgressions were sufficient to merit complete extinction but God through his mercies had saved a remnant. In keeping with God's concern and mercies each person should commit himself or herself completely to the worship and service of God. The people of the world may be cruel and unmerciful but God is compassionate and He does not fail. This places God above all other gods. Is God present to help us in trials and temptations?

Meditation: When our work in our present vocation fails guide us into another channel where we may continue to be of service. May I never fail to feel that God is with me! *Amen.*

August 3
THE CONTINUED CARE OF GOD

"They that wait for the Lord shall renew their strength, they shall mount up with wings like eagles, they shall run and not be weary, they shall walk and not faint." (Isaiah 40:31)

This description of God's constant care is marvelous. Strength may come through patience. It was clear to the prophet that the power of Babylon was coming to a close. The restoration of the remnant would be complete and He would continue to prove Himself the everlasting God. The strength and achievement of the remnant would lift like eagles wings. The fact is that Cyrus did give them an escort when they returned to Palestine. God proved to be their God and they returned with such joy that they may have felt that they were walking on air. God's spirit had supported their spirit and they began life with new vigor and determination.

Meditation: May the spirit that You gave us at our birth never fail! May we rejoice that You will carry us with the strength and assurance that the eaglets possess as the mother bird carries them safely. *Amen.*

August 4
THE INTIMACY OF GOD WHEN IN EXILE

"Can a woman forget her suckling child, that she should have no compassion on the son of her womb? Even these may forget, yet I will not forget you. Behold, I have graven you on the palms of my hands." (Isaiah 49:15-16)

As a mother is creative and becomes endeared to her child by the child being a part of herself, so God is endeared to us and we are a part of Himself. He is our Father-parent and a good father provides for his children. Hosea thought of God as a husband-marital love, and Isaiah thinks of Him as a parent-parental love. As a mother does not forget her child, so God did not forget them although they were in exile. Do we have need for a mother Goddess? What do you think of Mary, the mother of Jesus, as an intermediary? Should saints take the place of God?

Meditation: Help us to realize Your deep concern for us. As we cannot forget our children, so You will not forget us. You are the way, the truth and the life. We assume Your parenthood and accept Your fatherhood. *Amen.*

August 5
GOD'S CARE IS INCLUSIVE

"Turn to me and be saved, all the ends of the earth! For I am God, and there is no other." (Isaiah 45:22)

Here God is presented as the "go'el" or Redeemer of all people who will accept Him. For a time Cyrus, King of Persia, was God's agent to execute judgment upon Israel. This redemption and forgiveness was now being extended to people beyond Judah. Even the pagans had God's concern. This idea of the universality of God marks an important development. What do we mean when we say God is everywhere?

Meditation: Your intimacy startles us. What crisis should arise that would estrange us from You! The mother never forsakes her child but will sacrifice her strength and even herself. What a favor and uplift when we think and accept You on those terms! *Amen.*

August 6

THE UNIVERSAL REDEEMER

"He was wounded for our transgressions, he was bruised for our iniquities; upon him was the chastisement that made us whole, and with his stripes we are healed." (Isaiah 53:5)

Isaiah taught that God was the redeemer of the remnant and that the suffering, humiliation, sorrows, trials, disappointments and griefs were necessary to bring the people to themselves and to God. The chastisements were severe but Ezekiel and others were good pastors and the people repented, and turned to God as the primary Power of their devotion. This chastisement on the one hand and the endurance and patient conduct of the remnant on the other, they thought, may be an example that might even open the eyes of the pagans so that they might turn to God. The generosity of Cyrus seems to have given them a new insight of hope. The doors of the temple would be open for all to enter. Through their suffering and endurance the wounds were healed and health returned. *Meditation:* As a people of Yours may we sin less that we may suffer less! If other nations sin, let us remain faithful and it may come to pass that other nations that bring suffering upon us and upon themselves may be redeemed! *Amen.*

August 7

THE KNOWLEDGE OF THE SELF

"He shall see the fruit of the travail of his soul and be satisfied: by his knowledge shall the righteous one, my servant make many to be accounted righteous: and he shall bear their iniquities." (Isaiah 53:11)

This new principle in which suffering people may become

a medium to redeem other nations shows the importance of good shepherds when times are hard. Judah is pictured as God's missionary servant. God was proved trustworthy and through the conduct of Judah other nations were brought to God's care. Judah had learned that idol worship was useless. The pagan gods were powerless in contrast to the power of the God of the Hebrews.

Meditation: May we realize that our sufferings may not always be in vain. Keep us righteous and may we accept from You the rewards! *Amen.*

August 8
ZECHARIAH AND ETHICS

"Render true judgments, show kindness and mercy each to his brother, do not oppress the widow, the fatherless, the sojourner, or the poor; and let none of you devise evil against his brother in your heart." (Zechariah 7:9-10) (cf. Zechariah 8:16-17)

Zechariah reflects a Messianic era with hope. He never lost sight of the importance of the spiritual and ethical elements of conduct. He did not expect God to do all. Man should have proper conduct. Because the widow and orphan were at a disadvantage the tendency to take advantage of them was condemned. In fact it was a previous injunction to care for the widow and orphan but now it was a matter and conviction of the spirit. Notice that the last phrase "let none of you devise evil against your brother in his heart" is a negative statement of the Golden Rule in that the decision stems from the heart. Is the Golden Rule Christian, American or both?

Meditation: Let us, like Israel, discover for ourselves that conduct is the essence of religion. Help me to think of every person as Your child. *Amen.*

August 9
ISRAEL WILL HELP OTHER NATIONS

"Let us go with you, for we have heard that God is with you."
(Zechariah 8:23)

What a wonderful imagination! The prophet visioned
people of other nations coming to a Jew and asking if he
could go with him because he had heard that God was with
him. Even the pagan would be seeking better ways, better
companionship, better leadership and Judah had proved to
be the "apple of God's eye." (Zechariah 2:8c)

Meditation: We are grateful to think that God is with us to
help us. May he continue to use agents like Cyrus to encourage the faithful, and nations like Judah to exemplify
righteous conduct in the midst of depression and worry. As
a nation may we be united with other nations in saying with
Ruth "thy people shall be my people and thy God, my God."
Amen.

August 10
PROPER FASTING

*"Is it not to share your bread with the hungry, and bring the
homeless poor into your house; when you see the naked to
cover him, and not to hide yourself from your own flesh."*
(Isaiah 58:7)

To abolish former provincial customs was not easy. Was
fasting a worthy ritual? Does the provident God delight in
fasting as a ritual? Both Zechariah, and Haggai, as well as
Isaiah, believe the placation of wrongdoings with burnt offerings was an abomination. To please God is to share and not
to burn anything. The prophets of this era teach that heaven
is God's throne and earth his footstool. Haggai and Zechariah
felt that a temple was needed but agreed with Isaiah that
fasting was a pagan idea of pleasing or placating God.

Meditation: If we fast may it be to share with the hungry!

May the abundance of food possessed by one nation be shared with other nations! Help us to find an equitable way to do this. Generate in all people the spirit of being thankful when sharing! *Amen.*

August 11

THE MISSION OF ISRAEL

"The Spirit of the Lord God is upon me, because the Lord has anointed me to bring good tidings—to bind up the broken hearted, to proclaim liberty to the captives—the opening of the prison—to proclaim the year of the Lord's favor, and the day of vengeance of our God." (Isaiah 61:1-2)

The suffering and exile of Israel was not useless. The Spirit of the Lord God had been recognized and accepted. The people had a mission. The way of righteousness had been found. Vengeance was not a means for man to avenge a wrong in order to secure justice. This was something that belonged to the Creator. The joy of the righteous is the reward for noble acts. Jesus had found and adopted this as his first message in announcing his mission in the synagogue at Nazareth. He made this mission apply to himself and his acts fulfilled its philosophy. Will you make the above your mission? *Meditation:* We thank You that we are free to do right or to choose evil! May we follow the example of Jesus in choosing the good and making this our mission! *Amen.*

August 12

THE EFFECTIVENESS OF THE NEW COVENANT

"My spirit is upon you, and my words which I have put in your mouth, shall not depart out of your mouth . . . from this time forth and for evermore." (Isaiah 59:21)

To this Isaiah the new covenant contains the redeeming way of God. It will bring joy and peace. God is sovereign and both Jews and Gentiles will become shepherds of the people and priests of God. This fellowship of peace even extends to the animals. (Isaiah 11:6) God being among the people will cause them to seek justice and to love righteousness with the result that other people from distant lands will wish to come and learn about the mercy, justice and glory of God. Have you read the book of Isaiah and sensed the value of the new spiritual covenant? Is the spiritual covenant operative today? Do you think there is more than one author in the book of Isaiah?

Meditation: When the Spirit of God is with a person it gives peace that may be like the peace of a river on a calm and sunny day. May Your Spirit ever pour itself into me! *Amen.*

August 13

THE IDEAL HIGHWAY

"The redeemed shall walk there." (Isaiah 35:9c)

Isaiah, Chapters thirty-four and thirty-five, describe the ideal highway. In place of sorrow and sighing there shall be gladness and joy. The ransomed will return in joy. The weak will receive strength. Other nations will walk on it and it will be the highway of refuge. Fear shall depart for even the wild beast shall become domesticated. The goodness in mankind will bring kindness, forgiveness and peace. Does this Isaiah prepare the way for the life and teachings of Jesus?

Meditation: May the vision of Isaiah become a reality in our day! Let righteousness flow into the people so that all nations shall be exalted together! *Amen.*

August 14

THE CONSERVATIVES

"Moreover you shall accept no ransom for the life of a murderer who is guilty of death, but he shall be put to death." (Numbers 35:31)

Not all accepted the prophetic idea of God being the

avenger. There were conservatives who believed that the guilty should be punished at the testimony of witnesses. This was the priestly explanation of how to deal with the unsocial and wrongdoer. It is true that concern had moved out of the individual stage into the social when the books of Leviticus and Numbers were re-edited. The idea of limited revenge by society prevailed. The editing reflected the teachings that came out of the exile that were not completely prophetic. The new covenant idea had been born and it plagued the conservatives. How shall we deal today with people who are revengeful? What should be our method of dealing with the unsocial?

Meditation: We are thankful that the tendency to forgive and to love God and one's fellowmen is still at work. May the adherents of the new covenant increase so that wars shall end! *Amen.*

August 15

WHAT ABOUT EDOM

"As you have done, it shall be done to you." (Obadiah 15b) (cf Jeremiah 50:29)

At this period of time the conservatives held that the Edomites and Babylonians were doomed for destruction. The Edomites were descendants of Esau who had married outside the Israelite clan and therefore, were not descendants of the pure stock of Jacob. This party insisted that the "law of vengeance" should be mitigated but it should be along the order of "like for like." Do you know people who still hold to the conservative idea of revenge as the medium of dealing with criminals? Should punishment be punitive or educational?

Meditation: May we cease to be suspicious of the motives of another! May we be alert but not condemnatory, intelligent but not assertive, searchers but open and not secretive, strong but not dictatorial! *Amen.*

August 16

MALACHI IS HOPEFUL

"For you who fear my name, the sun of righteousness shall arise with healing in its wings." (Malachi 4:2)

Malachi means "my messenger" and as a prophet he is hopeful. Although he had both priestly and prophetic insights, he thought of God as Father. To him the moral law was valid and people would and should suffer for their transgressions. Those who accepted God and his righteousness were the righteous. God was merciful and the righteousness in persons would of itself have healing values. God is regarded as the healer of physical and spiritual wounds. Have you ever thought how the body responds with healing to an injury? The corpuscles rush to the injured place to heal. Can you think of spiritual resources that hasten to heal spiritual wounds?

Meditation: Help me to live so that I shall not wound the spirit of another. Let us work together to keep the spiritual scars minimal! *Amen.*

August 17

RELIGION IS OF THE HEART

"Where you go I will go, and where you lodge I will lodge, your people shall be my people and your God, my God." (Ruth 1:16cd)

The book of Ruth is evidently a late book in Jewish history. The purpose seems to have been that of a protest against the crusade that sanctioned marriage within the clan only. It teaches that even a Moabite may be blessed in that Ruth, a Moabitess, married Boaz, the descendant of Jesse, the father of David. It shows that intermarriage with a foreigner may not be so bad. It is a book with a protest against narrow nationalism. It teaches that God is interested in all people. Do you believe in mixed marriages?

Meditation: We thank You that the legalisms of the priestly party did not prevail over the covenant idea of relationship with Yourself. Help us to remember that we are all of one blood. *Amen.*

August 18
THE IDEA OF GOD BEING MERCIFUL PERSISTS

"Return unto the Lord, your God, for he is gracious and merciful, slow to anger, and abounding in steadfast love." (Joel 2:13)

Joel urged the people to turn to God with fasting and sacrifice. God would take them back, forgive them, reward the faithful and be gracious and merciful to them. He would prove to be a refuge and a stronghold. The writings of Joel are optimistic with high regard for the keeping of the covenant. The restoration seemed limited to Judah and Jerusalem and yet the outpouring of the Spirit seemed to be promised to all flesh. Peter thought the outpouring of the Spirit on the day of Pentecost was a fulfillment of Joel's insight. (Acts 2:16f) Do you feel that God's Spirit is being poured on you?

Meditation: May the visions of Joel give support to our occasional visions. Let us never forsake God or deny the covenant for we have the assurance that God will not forsake us! *Amen.*

August   19
PERSISTENT IDEAS OF REVENGE

"Make them days of fasting and gladness, days for sending choice portions to one another and gifts to the poor." (Esther 9:22d)

The book of Esther has little to contribute to our subject except to show that evil intent can boomerang and fall upon the one who devises human vengeance. The evil that Haman planned for the Jews turned upon himself and the feast of

Purim became a time of feasting, joy and sharing. The shift of events turned the intended slaughter of the Jews and the hanging of Mordecai to a feast and the hanging of Haman upon the gallows he had intended for Mordecai. One lesson is that vengeance among men destroys and that love and decency brings joy.

Meditation: Help us to keep in mind that this is Your world. We must learn to care for ourselves according to Your will. We believe that if we accept our sonship we shall never be forsaken. *Amen.*

August 20

DIVINE RETRIBUTION

"For the Lord your God is gracious and merciful." (2 Chronicles 30:9)

The books of Chronicles reflect the ideas of the priestly period. It no longer emphasizes "like for like" but divine retribution upon the unjust and reward and favor upon the just. The citadel of worship became the temple in Jerusalem. The thought prevailed that worship and loyalty to God would win favor. The theme seems to be that good kings prospered but bad kings were failures and caused Israel to transgress. It describes a time when it was thought that the descendants of Abraham were God's chosen people. Does God have special chosen people? Are we God's chosen people when we choose to accept and to do the will of God?

Meditation: May we be loyal to our religion but help us to be certain that our religion is of God and not mere provincialism. Let us work so that the prevailing custom of worship is grounded in the righteousness and love of God to all people! *Amen.*

August 21
GOD IS GOD OF ALL

"Thou art a gracious God and merciful, slow to anger, and abounding in steadfast love, and repentest of evil." (Jonah 4:2c)

The book of Jonah, which includes this sentence from Jonah's prayer, teaches the universality of God's care and love. The Ninevites were Gentiles but God would save them. Jonah might have been an effective speaker to convert the Ninevites and God needed him. The assumption is that evil destroys but repentance follows with righteousness to save all people including the Gentiles. Do not become involved in the whale incident so that you lose the point. It is a great book and teaches the love and care of God for all people. How many of us have had a whale of an experience?

Meditation: May we never lose sight of the fact that evil destroys and that righteousness builds. Let us remember that we are an important part of God's world! *Amen.*

August 22
GOD'S REGARD FOR GENTILES

"Should not I pity Nineveh." (Jonah 4:11a)

Jonah at the beginning is typical of the outlook and spirit of the Jewish people of a later period in Jewish history. Jonah disliked the Gentiles. Let them destroy themselves might have been his opinion. Through a whale experience he submitted to the call of God and began preaching to the Ninevites. The Ninevites responded, repented and the city was saved. The book teaches how God uses persons to call others to a sense of rightness. It summons Israel to its mission. A greater one than Jonah presented a similar message. Is there any similarity of Jonah's three days and three nights discomforture with the three days of Jesus in the tomb?

Meditation: Each of us has a mission. Let us live so that the fulfillment of each mission may dovetail into the love of God toward all people! *Amen.*

August 23

JOB'S COMFORT

"For I know that my Redeemer lives." (Job 19:25a)

A redeemer or "go'el" is a person who avenged a wrong. It was a primitive method for the sake of security. If a wrong or hurt had been committed to a member of a tribe or clan it was the duty of the next of kin to avenge the murder or wrong according to the degree defined by the mores of the tribe or clan. There were times when the injured tribe or clan would accept a ransom payment. The person or persons paying the ransom were named "redeemers." To Job, God was his redeemer and he committed himself to God. He had faith in God and was committed to His will. Does the surrender of Job to the will of God suggest anything to you about Jesus being a redeemer?

Meditation: May Jesus be my redeemer. He went to the cross because the sinful and misunderstanding people of His time placed him there. As He forgave them so He has forgiven me. *Amen.*

August 24

JOB'S INTEGRITY

"Is not . . . the integrity of your ways your hope?" (Job 4:6)

The answer to Eliphaz is, "Yes." The causes of suffering to the righteous as outlined by the book of Job are: first, a test; second, punitive; third, discipline; and fourth, mystery. The friends of Job tried to analyze his situation but none of them had a satisfactory solution. Vicarious suffering was not suggested but Job remained submissive for, although he could not comprehend the reason, he relied with childlike trust on God's wisdom and goodness. The book of Job opens the subject of suffering and, although it does not give an acceptable cause, it prepares the way for righteousness to be sustained and vicarious suffering or the way of the cross to give the answer.

Meditation: May I follow the pattern of Job if necessary. May suffering to me and my family be avoided by our righteous conduct and sound actions. But, if I have to suffer let it be with love! *Amen.*

August 25

THE BOOK OF PROVERBS

"The fear of the Lord is the beginning of knowledge." (Proverbs 1:7)

The text is the keynote of the book of Proverbs. To fear God is to have respect for his creatorship, goodness and greatness. When we think of the fear of God we hold that love for God is so deep and convincing that we are afraid to do wrong because it is an affront to God Who loves me and Whom I love. Love impels me so that I am afraid to do wrong. Do you think that the idea of the "fear of God" was a holdover from the time when people feared the god or gods and tried to placate or appease them with sacrifices? Why is there so much about the fear of God in the Old Testament and so much of the love and favor of God in the New Testament?

Meditation: We thank those who preserved for us the descriptions of the searchings for God. Since we have found God to be gracious and forgiving let us be faithful in serving Him! *Amen.*

August 26

NEIGHBORLINESS

"Do not plan evil against your neighbor." (Proverbs 3:29a)

The above weakens the "law of revenge" which had existed

for centuries. In a sense it is a negative statement of the
Golden Rule. Sometimes it requires intelligence not to plan
evil. The book of Proverbs grew out of the practical ways of
everyday living. It is a sort of Benjamin Franklin almanac.
While we do find some proverbs relating to revenge, yet for
our study there is much in them that favors the good neighbor
policy. Statements like "The Lord reproves him whom he
loves" (Proverbs 3:12) and "a friend loves at all times, and a
brother is born for adversity" (Proverbs 17:17) show that
love was regarded as an active human and divine force. Have
all people come to understand the real meaning of love? Is
love more than emotions? How many kinds of love can you
name?

Meditation: Keep us good neighbors wherever we may live.
Let mercy and truth prevail! May my neighborliness make
good neighbors! *Amen.*

August 27
KINDNESS TO OTHERS IS ENJOINED

*"If your enemy is hungry, give him bread to eat: and if he is
thirsty, give him water to drink; for you will heap coals of
fire on his head."* (Proverbs 25:21-22) (cf. Romans 12:20)

There are injunctions that one should never forsake kindness and truth, but keep these ideas intimate by writing them
on the tablet of the heart. The text urges kindness to an
enemy. Paul evidently thought it worked or he would not
have quoted it in Romans 12:20. This kind method of dealing with an enemy shames the enemy, makes him think deeply
and review his own actions and attitudes so that the blood in
response to his inward feeling reddens his countenance, and
warmth of the head and face follows. It is not the usual way
of treating an enemy, but by making him feel guilty it has
much value for our study. Do you remember how David
showed kindness to Saul at a time when he was an enemy

and Saul said "you are more righteous than I, for you have repaid me good, whereas, I have repaid you evil." (1 Samuel 24:17)

Meditation: May kindness prevail in me at all times. We are grateful that we live at a time when wrath and cruelty as a method of success has been proved faulty! *Amen.*

August 28

THE EVOLUTION OF LOVE

"For love is strong as death, jealousy is cruel as the grave. Its flashes are flashes of fire, a most vehement flame. Many waters cannot quench love, neither can floods drown it." (Song of Solomon 8:6-7a)

Parental love is strong, marital love is binding and filial love is natural. All were operative in Hebrew life and all are operative today. The earliest word for love was DOD. A stronger word is AHAB which suggests deep subjective love which projects itself upon the object as dutiful, sacrificial and kindly as it reaches toward its object in the Spirit of helpfulness. DOD and other words have the suggestion of possession and that is the weakest form of love. Real love is outgoing. Passionate or physical love is possession and it is transitory. Real love is eternal and always personal.

Meditation: Help me to love as human beings should. We thank You for the strength of love, the warmth, the eternity of love in that we never complete it here on earth. Keep me in the love of God! *Amen.*

August 29

THE PSALMS

"He makes a pit, digging it out, and falls into the hole which he has made." (Psalm 7:15)

The Psalms were the hymns of the period of the second temple. They express many shades of thought. The law of retaliation is reflected in some of them. Most of them reflect the law of love. Some enjoin the spirit of love toward a neighbor and others enjoin love toward all. Revenge, like the above text, sometimes describes man's vengeance like a man digging a pit and then falling into it himself. Psalm 137 expresses vengeance toward the Edomites but does not make good reading. Would you ever use Psalm 137 as a responsive reading in a worship service?

Meditation: The hardships in life may promote harshness of the spirit. Does captivity tend to create hatred against the captors or does it sometimes teach the values of kindness and forgiveness? May I be kind to my enemies and it may be that they will become my friends. *Amen.*

August 30

THE GOOD SHEPHERD

"The Lord is my shepherd, I shall not want, etc." (Psalms 23:1)

The Psalms have many phrases of endearment. There is constant repetition of God as merciful, full of loving kindness, praiseworthy, forgiving and deserving of worship. He is thought of as a good Shepherd in contrast with false shepherds. The idea of God leading his people as a shepherd leads his flock is a popular symbol. Do you suppose that Jesus got the idea of the parable of the good shepherd from his knowledge of this twenty-third Psalm? Read John 10:1-18 and Luke 15:3-7. God does not like to have anything lost.

Meditation: Keep us faithful to You as we want to be faithful in our vocations. May we never become lost from You for we know that You will never lose us. We are Thine; do Thou befriend us. Be the Guardian of our way. *Amen.*

August 31

GOD AS A REFUGE

"He will cover you with his pinions and under his wings you will find refuge; his faithfulness is a shield and buckler." (Psalms 91:4)

The picture of this Pilgrim Psalm is worth retaining. For God to hide us with his wings and under his feathers as the bird and chicken does is suggestive of God's parental care. It helped people to think of Him as Father rather than as a judge. A father tries to give righteous and fair judgment. While there may be chastisement, it is intended to develop the growing personality. God likes to think of us as continually growing. If heaven is the culmination of a good life then all of life must be a growing and expanding life. This makes regular worship and Bible study important for adults as well as children. As the bird or hen protects and warms the young with her own body so God supports and warms us with His Holy Spirit.

Meditation: Will You cover our sins and take them away. Cover them with righteous deeds and Your warm heart and it may be that the conscience will be healed. *Amen.*

September 1

LOVING KINDNESS ENDURES

"Bless the Lord . . . who heals all your diseases . . . who crowns you with steadfast love and mercy." (Psalm 103:2a)

The Hebrew word CHESED and its derivatives is often translated "loving kindness." It is used at least 127 times in the Psalms. Discussions have centered on whether it is used in the active sense of dutiful love to God or in the passive sense that defines the nation as the object of God's love. It is consistently used in the sense of "steadfast love." Is it God's steadfast love that prompts his forgiveness and the restoration of intimate relations? Is the love of God and man retroactive?

Meditation: We are grateful for the Psalms because they are comprehensive and show the searchings and findings of the Shepherd of the souls of men. *Amen.*

September 2

GOD IS RIGHTEOUS

"For the Lord is righteous, he loves righteous deeds." (Psalm 11:7a)

The righteous person finds it relatively easy to love God because it is his nature to love. Any person who has found God and retains His Spirit in his mind and heart has better control of himself than the one who has hatred. Love soothes. Hatred disturbs. Hatred, revenge and suspicion always suggest confusion and frustration. Are two great nations, the United States and Russia, disturbed right now? Is it because they are suspicious of each other?

Meditation: We have learned that righteousness and peace may kiss each other, and we believe that the joining of these intimate elements produce the abundant and contented life. Help me to live the abundant life today and every day! *Amen.*

September 3

GOD KEEPS THE COVENANT

"O Lord, the great and terrible God, who keepeth covenant and steadfast love with those who love him and keep his commandments." (Daniel 9:4b)

The book of Daniel was written in a time of persecution to show that God is in control and that He will preserve the righteous and faithful. Tyrants hold their places in the world only by the grace of God but their power is nebulous. Nebuchadnezzar, king of Babylon, was warned that his kingdom was uncertain, and near the end of his life he, being in distress and humiliation, admitted to the Most High that His kingdom was an everlasting dominion. (Daniel 4:34) The consistency in proclaiming God as powerful, righteous and a keeper of the covenant is proverbial throughout most of the Old Testament. Do you think that God is working purposely now? Is the time urgent that Christians should rethink their notion of Jesus and of God?

Meditation: That Daniel prayed for the repentance of his enemies teaches the power of prayer. The fact that Daniel and the three Hebrew children were saved from terrible situations should stimulate us to fervent prayer. Let us, as a nation, resort to prayer and have less faith in the sword! *Amen.*

September 4
IMMORTALITY AND THE FAITHFUL

"And those who are wise shall shine like the brightness of the firmament; and those who turn many to righteousness, like the stars for ever and ever." (Daniel 12:3)

The conviction persisted that God was supreme; the wicked will be punished within their own wickedness. The fact that Daniel received protection, compassion and survived was a strong factor in retaining faith in doing good rather than evil. Even Darius, the king of Persia, who asked, "Is Thy God, whom thou servest consistently, able to deliver thee from the lions?" (Daniel 6:20), found the answer to be, yes. Daniel was delivered. The three Hebrews were not burned by the firey furnace. The idea of God's care gives evidence of a belief in immortality for the righteous. Do we have a need for immortality? Why?

Meditation: May we continue to believe that through righteousness the righteous shall survive and find a continued abode with God forever! *Amen.*

September 5
BREAD IS RETURNED

"Cast your bread upon the waters, for you will find it after many days." (Ecclesiastes 11:1)
"Remember, also your Creator in the days of your youth." (Ecclesiastes 12:1)

As we leave the Old Testament we are reminded of the philosophic teachings in it. The author of Ecclesiastes had a philosophy so extravagant that he believed that kindness scattered anywhere would be appreciated and returned. Another philosophic insight was that we should assume God, keep Him in the heart and mind in youth as well as in mature years. The idea of sowing wild oats is not consistent with the teaching of eternal love. Love is sacred, holy, supreme in value and should not be trifled with or desecrated. Since we are persons we can think only of God as a loving personality. The best gift to each person is the personality of God. Regardless of our facial expression or bodily contour each person is beautiful if the character is righteous. Do we need more make-up or more make-in?

Meditation: Let us assume God is our youth and then we will always have Him. Jesus assumed God and God became the basis of his power and his philosophy about life. *Amen.*

September 6
GOD OF THE PEOPLE

"And they shall be my people and I will be their God, in faithfulness and in righteousness." (Zechariah 8:8b)

The outlook of Jeremiah is echoed in the book of Zechariah. God is thought of as Protector, Shepherd, Redeemer, Defender and Saviour. The Messianic idea is somewhat vague. Was the Messianic King to be a destroyer or one that was meek and lowly and from the peasant class? The certainty persists that God is the rewarder of those who diligently seek Him; He delights in simple acts like giving a drink of water, handing bread to another and continued devotion.

Meditation: As the canon of the Old Testament closes, hope in the power of God, faith in the love of God, the certainty of the mercy of God and the eternity of God is basic. May faith, hope and love prevail in me. *Amen.*

September 7

A NEGATIVE STATEMENT OF THE GOLDEN RULE

"And what thou thyself hatest, do to no man." (Tobit 4:16-17)

The intertestamental literature may have helped to keep alive the concepts and viewpoints about God and His dealing with people. The intervening years between the writings that closed the canon of the Old Testament and the assembling of the New Testament writings had active individuals and sects at work. Priestly orders were active in teaching and the Temple in Jerusalem was a center of worship for the Jews. This period may have had a value in teaching and bringing certain forms of ethics into the New Testament. Men were taught to be righteous as God was righteous. Marriage was regarded as sacred and love and respect for parents were repeatedly taught and practiced.

Meditation: May the teaching of the Old Testament continue to help us to comprehend the problems of the New. May our worship of God continue. Help us to teach and to know the Words of God aright! *Amen.*

September 8

ECCLESIASTICUS

"He that revengeth shall find vengeance from the Lord." (Ecclesiasticus 28:1)

The proverbs, maxims and rules of conduct in this book are typical of many others of the period. The book of Sirach holds that man's wisdom may approximate divine wisdom to the faithful and loyal Israelite. The book of Jubilee often repeats that God will show mercy and forgiveness to all who seek it and that the high day of forgiveness is the day of Atonement.

Meditation: May we atone daily, hourly and minute by minute for our sins. May we know what charity is and to whom it should righteously and worthily be given. May forgiveness be a discipline for us! *Amen.*

September 9
THE TESTIMONY OF THE PATRIARCHS

"Love each one his brother with a good heart and the spirit of envy will withdraw from you." (Testimony of the Patriarchs 4:4-7)

The continual repetition in speech and in writings about the patriarchs and prophets helped to keep alive the concepts of God that were most vital. In spite of the spiritual phases of worship and loyalties to God, the priests continued to teach and to advocate formal worship and legal injunctions. The emphasis of the priests tended to create divisions and sects, like the Pharisees, Essenes, etc. The persistence of envy may have led to the philosophy of our text wherein love at work toward our fellowmen will cause envy to disappear or to be covered by good deeds toward others. Why do you think that conservative concepts persisted?

Meditation: May the teachings of the prophets prevail and the help that comes by regarding Jesus as Messiah, Saviour, Redeemer and Prophet increase our faith and assurance. Comfort us in trial as You comforted Joseph! *Amen.*

September 10

THE FOURTH MACCABEES

"How may I express the passionate love of parents for children." (4 Maccabees 15:4)

The parents of the seven Maccabee sons taught their children to be loyal to God. The mother saw several of her sons horribly mangled and put to death but she never lost her faith in the power of God to vindicate the wrong. That these parents and children were supported by inspired reason seems to have been a philosophical explanation about how they could endure so much and still remain faithful. The inter-testamental literature has value but it leaves room for the revelation of God through the life and teachings of Jesus, who gave the assurance of Divine Love being fulfilled through Him. The highway of love and righteousness is prepared for Jesus by the Maccabees, John the Baptist and others.

Meditation: May the convictions and worthy lives of the Maccabees inspire us to be faithful witnesses to the Spirit of God in history! *Amen.*

September 11

THE NEW TESTAMENT

"Repent, for the kingdom of heaven is at hand." (Matthew 3:2)

There is much in common in the synoptic Gospels of Matthew, Mark and Luke. Matthew and Luke depend largely on Mark and it is generally agreed that Mark was the earliest of the written Gospels. God was thought to be in control and John the Baptist alerted the people that the kingdom of heaven was at hand. Repentance involves the admission of sin and its forgiveness. John's idea of the kingdom of heaven was the spiritual reign of God in the minds and conduct of the people. What do you think the kingdom of heaven is?

Meditation: "The light of God is falling Upon life's common
way;

We hear thy true voice leading Our song of
brotherhood."

lines from Hymn by Louis F. Benson

September 12
WHAT REPENTANCE INVOLVES

*"He who has two coats, let him share with him who has none;
and he who has food, let him do likewise."* (Luke 3:11)

John the Baptist presented his mission by quoting from
Isaiah (Isaiah 40:3f) and then anticipated that someone
would remind him that they were not so bad in that they
were descendants of Abraham. Having explained the useless-
ness of that boast the people asked what they should do. John
responded by citing ethical needs for sharing of garments and
food. The preparation for the kingdom was not a formal
need but the outgoing of the spirit of man to man in sharing
as there was need. Do you agree with John's citation of the
ethical need for sharing?

Meditation: "The voice of God is calling Its summons unto
men;

Whom shall I send to succor My people in their
need?"

lines from Hymn by John Haynes Holmes

September 13
THE WAY OF THE LORD

"Prepare the way of the Lord." (Luke 3:4c)
"All flesh shall see the salvation of God." (Luke 3:6)

This quotation from Isaiah 40:3-5 shows the stream of
thought running through the Old Testament into the New.
For centuries the idea of a Messiah or "anointed One of God"
ran like an irregular stream through the generations. John

proclaimed that the long wished for era was present and advised the people to repent, get into the stream of ethical traffic and straighten the spiritual highway. This was the time. The highway was one of righteousness and the preparation had already begun. Do you think that John the Baptist was efficient in preparing the way for Jesus?

Meditation: We thank You that John proclaimed the task as urgent, the way leading through valleys was crooked and it was the duty of the people to pitch in to make the highway straight and the road high. *Amen.*

September 14

THE QUESTION OF THE MESSIAH

"The people were in expectation, and all men questioned in their hearts concerning John, whether, perhaps, he were the Christ." (Luke 3:15)

The efficiency and message of John aroused the curiosity of the people. Some thought that he, himself, might be the Messiah (Hebrew), Christ (Greek). John was definite in replying that he was not the Christ but the forerunner. He would baptize with water, whereas Christ would baptize with the Holy Spirit. The judgment of Christ would be factual. The immediate need was repentance and a determining factor in judgment would be the fruitage. What fruit am I bearing? Are you and I just chaff?

Meditation: May I, like John, proclaim the acceptable year of the Lord and that the year is this year, the land is this land and the person is myself. Do I have a message as pertinent and imperative as that of John? *Amen.*

September 15

JESUS IS SUBJECT TO HIS PARENTS

"Glory to God in the highest, and on earth peace among men with whom he is pleased." (Luke 2:14)

The reported message of the angels is pertinent to our study. When Jesus was born God was praised and glorified by the angels closest to Him who said that peace as an objective would prevail among the people of the earth who were righteous and in tune with the Creator. This insight inspired shepherds to go to Bethlehem to announce the birth of Jesus to the world, and wise men to travel long and far with gifts. For many a new spiritual era had begun. For others it was a concern and even Herod became suspicious. The parents outwitted King Herod by their urge to care and save the child. Jesus lived with his parents at Nazareth, studied the Scriptures and made journeys with them to the temple in Jerusalem.

Meditation: We are grateful that Luke has recorded Jesus' concern for the teachings about God and received inspiration and insight from the teachers as he listened and asked questions in the temple at Jerusalem. *Amen.*

September 16

JESUS IS BAPTIZED

"For thus it is fitting for us to fulfill all righteousness." (Matthew 3:15c)

John's preaching about the need of good ethics in preparation for entrance into the kingdom attracted many people. Finally Jesus came among them and was welcomed by John with the words "Behold the Lamb of God." (John 1:29b) The request of Jesus for baptism according to Jesus' own words was to fulfill righteousness. Righteousness and the proclaiming of it was Jesus' mission. Read the chapters about his early life. Luke 2:39-52 gives a concise description.

Meditation: May we, like Jesus, be subject to You! May we make as our aim the fulfilling of righteousness! Begin with me now. *Amen.*

September 17
WORSHIP IS STRONGER THAN TEMPTATION

"You shall worship the Lord your God and him only shall you serve." (Matthew 4:10b)

Three tests show the power and control of Jesus upon Whom had come the Holy Spirit with the dove as a witness; the first or physical temptation was disposed of by a quotation Scripture; the second or intellectual was flouted by an equally appropriate Scripture; the third or spiritual and last brought forth from Jesus the content of the first of the Ten Commandments in that there was only one God worthy of worship. The consistency of Jesus' answers and the supreme place he gave to the worship of God floored Satan and he disappeared. Jesus had entered into the New Covenant, for in both the Old and the New Covenants the worship of God is primary. Will worship disperse Satan and the imps of temptation today?

Meditation: We learn from the record of Jesus' temptations the importance of Scripture as a bulwark against temptation. Let us be like Jesus and consistently worship God and it may be that the Scripture we learn in worship will be a fortress to us. *Amen.*

September 18
JESUS IN THE SYNAGOGUE OF NAZARETH

"The Spirit of the Lord is upon me, because he has anointed me to preach good news to the poor, etc." (Luke 4:18-19)

This is another Scripture quotation. It is Isaiah 61:1-2 and it may not have been incidental that Jesus was given this section of the Scripture scroll to read. In any case he accepted it as his mission and applied it to himself and said "Today this scripture has been fulfilled in your hearing." (Luke 4:21) This Scripture should be read often. Like Jesus we should make and think of the Scripture applying to ourselves. Much of history is embodied in the Bible and we need to learn the power of righteousness and the weakness of evil. Do you think Jesus selected this Scripture or was it incidental?

Meditation: Teach us how to apply the Scripture to ourselves. May we compare our mission and place in life with the teachings of Jesus! *Amen.*

September 19
FULFILLMENT OF SCRIPTURE

"Today this scripture has been fulfilled in your hearing." (Luke 4:21c)

Jesus felt that he had a mission that fulfilled Scripture in that he was anointed (Messiah means anointed) to preach the gospel to the poor, to proclaim release to the captives, recovering of sight to the blind, set at liberty those who are oppressed and to proclaim the acceptable year of the Lord. It may be noted that Luke does not include the words of Isaiah 61:2b "the day of vengeance of our God." (cf. Isaiah 61:1-3) Is this a conclusive proof that Jesus regarded God as love to be primary Do you believe that since we think of God as love He is not a God of vengeance? Is cosmos itself the only vengeful force? Does vengeance suggest judgment?

Meditation: Help us to try to fulfill Scripture! Help us to feel that if we conscientiously worship God and do our vocational work well we fulfill Scripture. *Amen.*

September 20
UNRIGHTEOUSNESS IS CONDEMNED

"The scribes and Pharisees sit in Moses' seat . . . they preach but they do not practice. They bind heavy burdens . . . and lay them on men's shoulders." (Matthew 23:2, 3b, 4ab)

The insight of Jesus revealed that the scribes and Pharisees of his day were unscrupulous, legalistic, liked pre-eminent places, coveted distinction and were, therefore, hypocritical and inconsistent with the spiritual covenant. This sort of conduct was not in accordance with the teachings of the patriarchs, the prophets or authors of many Psalms. Within the discipleship of Jesus there was no distinction as to wealth, color, caste or occupation. Each was called to serve worthily within the principles of righteousness. Were some of the disciples over amibitious?

Meditation: May our ideas of righteousness be simple, definite and in keeping with our own particular talent and mission! *Amen.*

September 21

THE FOURTH WOE

"Woe to you, scribes and Pharisees, hypocrites! for you tithe mint and dill and cummin, and have neglected the weightier matters of the law, justice, mercy and faith." (Matthew 23:23)

This is the fourth of the seven denunciations. Laws are not wrong in themselves but if they are a substitute for right and fairness they are worse than useless. The meticulous concern for tithing had obstructed justice, mercy and faith. Justice, a passion to establish righteousness, mercy, the mightiest of the mighty, loving sympathy, faith and staunch loyalty to principle are positive elements that were being smothered by devotion to material details. Were these unethical practices followed on the grounds of good business?

Meditation: May the weightier matters of the moral law take precedence over everything else! As we like justice, mercy and faith in others so we should practice and implement them ourselves. *Amen.*

September 22

A WRONG PRACTICE PRESAGES TROUBLE

"All this will come upon this generation." (Matthew 23:36)

The principle back of the denunciations was the neglect of privileges proffered by God. Luke thinks (Luke 11:49) that it was the wisdom of God to provide for man, send prophets, etc., but this wisdom was being spurned. Jesus seemed to think that the universe itself with its moral order would bring disaster because the primary principles of good teaching and living were being ignored. Future events seem to prove that Jesus' prophecy was correct, for social and religious conditions continued to grow worse. It was around 70 A.D. that Titus and his generals captured Jerusalem and destroyed the temple which has never been rebuilt. Why did the leaders continue to ignore basic principles?

Meditation: Let us exalt God together. We know through history that the ignoring of God and the failure to worship and obey His creative principles brought additional troubles. Make us strong to do Your will! *Amen.*

September 23
THE KEY OF KNOWLEDGE

"Woe to you lawyers! for you have taken away the key of knowledge: you did not enter yourselves and you hindered those who were entering." (Luke 11:52)

What a condemnation! The interpretation seems to be that the lawyers discouraged learning. They did not want the average person to have knowledge to discover what they themselves lacked. The laws within the field of religion failed to promote and sustain the important elements of justice, mercy and faith. Would you lock valuables in a chest or closet and then destroy the key? To set up false assumptions of truth will always boomerang. What ways do you suggest to spread the knowledge that Jesus taught? How may we improve our church schools?

Meditation: May we not be like the opponents of Jesus who had opportunities but failed to repent and change bad methods into good ones. May I never mislead another or deprive anyone of true knowledge! *Amen.*

September 24
THE GENERATION IN JEOPARDY

"The blood of all the prophets, shed from the foundation of the world, may be required of this generation." (Luke 11:50)

The overthrow of Jerusalem in 70 A.D. gives historical justification to the law of retribution. God did not want to destroy Jerusalem or the temple but their misuse made them an abuse and the Jews became a target for the Romans and their weakness an easy prey. A greater one than Jonah was in their midst but the leaders would not repent or accept him. With Jesus in their midst they had more possibilities for growth and salvation than the Ninevites in the time of Jonah. Do you think the rejection of righteous men and righteous ways condemned them?

Meditation: We are not our own. We are God's children. He has taught us the ways of salvation through Jesus and other prophets. May we walk in the way we know and obey the Christ we may know! *Amen.*

September 25
A BETRAYER DESTROYS HIMSELF

"Woe to that man by whom the Son of man is betrayed!" (Mark 14:21)

The betrayer of a good man betrays his best self with the result that he is his own destroyer. To have knowledge and not to use it is to betray knowledge and destroy it. Judas shared the life and teachings of Jesus just as did the other disciples. Because of his betrayal he suffered remorse, became frustrated and destroyed himself. Is this cosmic vengeance at its best? Judas by his own choice separated himself from communion with Christ and the fellowship of the disciples.

His own betrayal condemned him and life itself became un-bearable. Judas made a wrong choice. Those who conspired with Judas to betray Jesus became betrayers of Judas. Do you think Jesus at the Last Supper had compassion and pity for Judas?

Meditation: Our Father, we have been taught that wrong-doing betrays and punishes the wrongdoer. We do not ask You to help the wicked unless he repents but we do ask You to help the righteous and to keep them strong in their righteousness! *Amen.*

September 26
RIGHTEOUSNESS AND THE KINGDOM OF HEAVEN ARE SYNONOMOUS

"Unless your righteousness exceeds that of the scribes and Pharisees, you will never enter the kingdom of heaven." (Matthew 5:20)

After Jesus gave the principles for blessedness he called the attention of the disciples that the scribes and Pharisees were not following these rules. Righteousness flows from the heart and mind of man, is spiritual and within the plan of creation. A wrong motive fosters a wrong deed. To think evil has the moral effect of being evil. The will of God and the commandments are still operative.

Meditation: May right motives prevail in my heart! May my standard of self analysis come from You and not be confined to the standard of man! *Amen.*

September 27
UNBROTHERLINESS IS CONDEMNED

"Everyone who is angry with his brother shall be liable to the judgment; whoever insults his brother shall be liable to the council." (Matthew 5:22ab)

Some manuscripts have "without cause" inserted after the

word judgment. The family is the unit of happiness and any unbrotherliness is contrary to the divine plan and, therefore, contrary to the proper conduct of man in his relation with his fellowmen. Anger tends to create spiritual as well as physical wounds and in healing may leave scars. There are spiritual wounds and there are spiritual scars. We should be as careful not to wound the spirit of another as we are careful not to make a physical wound. Is it uncontrolled anger that causes wounds? Is anger ever justifiable? Can we have controlled anger?

Meditation: May we help our brother. If he is unjust then his injustice will fall upon his own head. Help me to be just and brotherly always! *Amen.*

September 28
GIFTS DO NOT ATONE FOR UNBROTHERLINESS

"Leave your gift before the altar and go; first be reconciled to your brother, and then come and offer your gift." (Matthew 5:24)

Evil merits punishment. Even a gift offered in worship with a spirit of unbrotherliness in the heart and mind is valueless. To make a gift effective one must be reconciled in heart and mind with the offended. It is a duty to settle one's account spiritually with another lest he himself should come into judgment. Can one pay money to receive forgiveness? Is forgiveness and reconciliation with another a spiritual adjustment?

Meditation: "Lord, to me compassion show. As thy tender mercies flow;

In thy vast and boundless grace. My transgressions all erase."

Psalm 51 from United Presbyterian
Book of Psalms

September 29

LOVE YOUR ENEMIES

"Love your enemies and pray for those who persecute you."
(Matthew 5:44)

According to the Sermon on the Mount, love toward an enemy is not casual. Love is an element that seeks good on all levels. Even if an enemy persecutes he should be prayed for. It is the difficult areas of the spirit that bother us. It is relatively easy to forgive and to pray for a friend. God has to deal with the recalcitrant and so do we. God does not strike down the offender but tries to save and recover him. It is difficult to befriend an enemy but to make a friend of an enemy is the greater good. Did Jesus win the friendship of the one on the cross? Do you find it difficult to forgive one who has harmed you or damned you with faint praise?

Meditation: "What a Friend we have in Jesus. All our sins
           and griefs to bear!
           What a privilege to carry Everything to God
           in prayer!"

                    from Hymn by Joseph Scriven

September 30

JUDGMENT OF OTHERS RETROACTIVE

"Judge not, that you be not judged." (Matthew 7:1) (cf. Luke 6:27)

The divine judgment is always upon us. One should be more critical of himself than of others. To make oneself a censor over the conduct of others is problematic. We can never know completely the other person's environment, experiences, education, outlook, opportunities, etc. God knows these things but we are limited in our knowledge. Therefore, it is better to let judgment be with God and His universal plan of judgment.

Meditation: May I constantly judge myself. I will be busy

enough for there is much that I lack. Let me not spend time in judging others lest I misuse my own time! *Amen.*

October 1
A LOG IN THE EYE

"First take the log out of your own eye, and then you will see clearly to take out the speck that is in your brother's eye." (Luke 6:42)

This is a splendid reference to a common ailment; we presume to judge others when our own judgment about ourselves is faulty. Judgment requires proper perspective if it is to be helpful. If one is psychologically defective he cannot be of much help to another. We cannot remove a speck from the eye of another when we have a larger substance in our own eye. We should try to develop in ourselves basic principles that will guide us in handling details. There are basic standards set up for us and if we have them well in mind we can help others. What was the basis of Jesus' judgment when he drove the money changers, etc., out of the temple? Was the basic principle—the temple is a house of prayer? Could Jesus see that it was not being used as a house of prayer?
Meditation: Help us to have standards of judgment like Jesus had. Judgment should be pivoted on—Is this right? Is it of God? Judgment can only be judgment when it is related to God's standards. Forgive us when we judge wrongly. *Amen.*

October 2
PARABLES OF JUDGMENT

"The field is the world, and the good seed means the sons of the kingdom; the weeds are the sons of the evil one." (Matthew 13:38)

The parables of the tares, drag-net and rich young man are practical teachings to show the constant judgment of God. How well are we using the resources of the kingdom! Are we prepared to meet the conditions of the kingdom? The standard of spiritual rightness is set up and we are free to conform or to rebel against it. If we conform, we make progress. If we rebel we nullify, delay or hinder the progress of righteousness. What is ethical rightness?

Meditation: Help us to be prepared for Your judgment at all times. Let us remember that the seeds of righteousness are available and then let us plant them freely like Johnny Appleseed nee: John Chapman. *Amen.*

October 3
WHEN MEN JUSTIFY THEMSELVES

"You are those who justify yourselves before men, but God knows your hearts; for what is exalted among men is an abomination in the sight of God." (Luke 16:15)

The parables of the unjust steward, and the rich man and Lazarus are examples of the folly of trusting in riches rather than in God. (Luke 16:19f) The rich man does not question the justness of his misery but shows his wordly technique in trying to find a way to warn his friends. The misuse of opportunities and responsibilities that riches offer is what is abominable. Wealth, a substitute for faith, justice and mercy, is what seems to have brought Dives into his sad state, whereas Lazarus, who seems to have fulfilled faith, justice and mercy, was justified in his future award. Did Jesus think man should be his own judge?

Meditation: Help us to be good and faithful stewards whether we have much or little. Help me to help others to help themselves in faith, justice and mercy! *Amen.*

October 4
WHEN MAN'S JUDGMENT IS WRONG

"And why do you not judge for yourselves what is right?" (Luke 12:57)

The reply of Jesus to the man who asked Jesus to direct his brother to divide the inheritance shows that Jesus did not regard himself as a judge of earthly possessions. They had their own judges. If the human mind under God is capable of making practical judgments of economic and social levels it should be used. Individuals exercise intelligence and judgment in considering weather conditions. Then why not rely on them and God's plan to decide economic and social levels. Can we be justified in submitting our problems to the judges of the land? Why not use prayer, reason, intelligence and the Spirit of God and settle our own problems?

Meditation: In our daily social affairs we have to make decisions. May we accustom ourselves to solve them with the spirit of God and the standards of righteousness and it may be that doing right will become automatic. *Amen.*

October 5

THE DISCIPLES REBUKED

"And when his disciples James and John saw it they said, 'Lord do you want us to bid fire come down from heaven and consume them?' " (Luke 9:54)

The disciples erred in attempting to judge the Samaritans when they were not welcomed into their cities. They had not yet learned that all people are God's people. They would have used the ancient method of revenge. They would have had Jesus use his power to destroy. Jesus' power, they should have known, was used to save, to heal and to build. The disciples learned later. They deserved the rebuke. The experience of Jesus at Sychar, a Samaritan village, was constructive and he was welcomed and did much good. Do you suppose Jesus' visit to Sychar was earlier than this experience of the disciples with the Samaritans? (see John 4:1-42)

Meditation: May discipleship in our day embody the comprehension and acceptance of the Spirit of God as interpreted by Jesus! *Amen.*

October 6
NOT ALL SUFFERING IS CAUSED BY SIN

"Unless you repent you will all likewise perish." (Luke 13:3)

The question arose whether the Galileans who were killed in Pilate's time and the eighteen upon whom the tower of Siloam fell were worse sinners than others. The answer Jesus gave was "No." Jesus brushed off the details of the incidents and generalized by saying that repentance was the issue of the hour for all. They needed to rethink the problem of accidents. Do you think the tower of Siloam was poorly constructed and that the calamity was vicarious because workmen had failed to construct a safe tower? Suffering may be caused through accident, failure of others to do good work, the sin of the self and the sins of others. The safe way is for all to accept the principles of the kingdom of God. What relation has an accident to sin? Are there accidents in nature?

Meditation: Help us to comprehend the will of God! May we not attribute to God mistakes that we ourselves have made! *Amen.*

October 7
THE PHARISEES ERRED IN JUDGMENT

"Cut it down; why should it use up the ground?" (Luke 13:7b)

The withering of the fig tree (Mark 11:12-24) (Matthew 21:18, 19) gave Jesus an opportunity to show a fault without hurting anyone. The lesson of the withered fig tree is that we will all perish unless we bear fruit. It is the duty of the gardener to nurture the trees and plants so they will flower and bear fruit. But if the gardener fails in his task the tree has no right to take up the ground space. Another tree and perhaps another kind can be planted in the same area. The fruit of the kingdom is to be righteous and just and if we do not produce these elements we are a nuisance to the kingdom. Bearing fruit means productiveness. Being God's covenant people we have a mission. What is your own mission? Am I producing fruits of righteousness?

Meditation: Make me fruitful in doing right for the sake of righteousness itself! It is better to walk in the right way than in the wrong way. Help me and keep me in the right way! *Amen.*

October 8

RELIGIOUS INSIGHT A DECIDING FACTOR

"Two men will be in the field; one is taken and one is left." (Matthew 24:40)

"Two women will be grinding at the mill; one is taken and one is left." (Matthew 24:41)

The nature of correct judgment depends on the religious and ethical insight. Two may work at the same trade and one may like it and the other may not. Which of the two will do the better work? Will a foreman see any difference in the production capacity of the two men? Will those who have special talents be given added responsibility and added returns?

Meditation: Take away doubt and unbelief. In the kingdom of God each one of us is judged independently. May I be certain that I am in the kingdom now. May the fruit I produce give evidence of spiritual health! *Amen.*

October 9

A STANDARD OF JUDGMENT

"I was hungry and you gave me food. I was thirsty and you gave me drink. I was a stranger and you welcomed me. I was

naked and you clothed me. I was sick and you visited me. I was in prison and you came to me." (Matthew 25:35-36)

Here is what might be called the trinity of love defined. We have love to God, love of God to man and love of man to man. It would almost seem as if the person had been generous so often that spontaneous loving service was given as a matter of course and there was no expectation of return. There were no qualifications or conditions as to place or circumstance. They show a general standard of action with love working with love of man to man, man to God and God to man. Will you define love in your own words?

Meditation: If we fulfill the principles of the Golden Rule the habit of doing good to others may become automatic. Just as baseball players think so much about the game and practice so much that their actions become reflex so may the doing of good works become automatic in us! *Amen.*

October 10
WHAT WE DO FOR PEOPLE WE DO FOR GOD

"Truly I say to you, as you did it to one of the least of these, my brethren, you did it to me." (Matthew 25:40)

Our future relationship with God depends on the way we deal with others. Doing well to others is doing well for God, and at the same time strengthens the self or personality of the doer. There is vicarious sinfulness. If we do good to another we help him, glorify God and edify ourselves. What is the result if we fail to do good and to help others? Could we be thrust out of the kingdom by our own deeds?

Meditation: To do for others makes us at one with our fellowmen. To help others is what a person should do for the common good. To be useful is to make Your work of perfecting righteousness our own. May our hearts and minds go out in love and sympathy toward all whose faith is assailed by doubt! *Amen.*

October 11

ENDURANCE IS THE TEST

"But he who endures to the end will be saved." (Matthew 10:22)

The test of living is not by spasmodic acts but by concrete deeds. We are not promised ease, health or freedom from accident. We are promised salvation as the reward of a good life. A time of judgment is the present. The sum of the series of deeds in each present time determines the final judgment. Endurance is a spiritual quality and the ability to keep love foremost as the method of righteousness is the goal of each endeavor. Jesus said "seek first his kingdom and his righteousness, and all these things shall be yours as well." (Matthew 6:33)

Meditation: Let not persecution, slights, misjudgments, misunderstandings or anything else make us bitter toward others or toward You. Let us act as if we believe that God is the rewarder of those who diligently seek Him. *Amen.*

October 12

ABOMINATION OF DESOLATION

"But when you see Jerusalem surrounded by armies, then know that the desolation has come here." (Luke 21:20)

Jerusalem was captured by the Syrians in the time of Antiochus Epiphanes about 170 B.C. He did not hesitate to introduce pagan worship. Jesus and others were probably familiar with that history. Would it occur again! The Jews had many setbacks but a remnant survived and restoration followed. The Jews were accustomed to philosophize about history and Jesus seemed to think that their rejection of him as the Messiah would bring desolation. As a matter of fact it did. Were these times of desolation the judgment of God or a matter of persons and nations within the world itself?

Meditation: Jesus seemed to hold that the leaders of the

Jewish people were missing an opportunity when they rejected Him. But, like a faithful son of the nation, He remained loyal to his principles and hoped for a time of redemption. *Amen.*

October 13

THE SEAT OF POWER

"Hereafter, you will see the Son of man seated at the right hand of Power and coming on the clouds of heaven." (Matthew 26:64)

This statement of Jesus seems to show that judgment is not a single event. It seems to assume that Jesus, Himself, had influence in heaven and that this influence reached to the people of the earth. Was the crucifixion to be an end of the legal period, with members of the Sanhedrin among the judges, or the beginning of a spiritual kingdom wherein men and women will have inherent judgment as to what is of God and what is not? Does this suggest that the Spirit of Jesus or that Jesus, Himself, will have some part in the final judgment? Can any earthly person assign the soul of man to heaven or to hell? Is judgment in God's hands?

Meditation: Having the standard of judgment in us let us use it. Let us seek the kingdom of God and His righteousness and trust to the future for judgment. *Amen.*

October 14

THIS GENERATION

"This generation will not pass away before all these things take place." (Mark 13:30)

The generation in which Jesus lived was an important one. The generation in which we live has urgent needs. For a time Judaism was an obstacle to the spread of the message of the kingdom. Although Jews persecuted the Christians in the days of Stephen and Paul, Gentile as well as Jewish churches were organized. What the Gentiles were doing the Jews should have been doing. In the midst of the divisions, Titus, the Roman general, attacked and captured Jerusalem and destroyed the temple in 70 A.D. Dispersion of Judaism came in that generation. Jesus was right. Did the fall of Jerusalem scatter the Jews?

Meditation: We do not pray for calamity, but if we are so stupid that we will not receive and do the work of a Christian we, too, shall become weak and another nation or nations will become agents of God to bring us to our senses. May we repent and serve You now. *Amen.*

October 15

THE VENGEANCE OF GOD

"For these are days of vengeance, to fulfill all that is written." (Luke 21:22)

How should the siege and overthrow of Jerusalem by Titus be analyzed? Was it the rejection of Jesus that led to division, frustration and weakness? What were the contributing factors? Did the first Christians attribute the fall of the city to the rejection of good, the perpetuation of Phariseeism, persecution, stubbornness and hard-heartedness? They had not kept the covenant or the Ten Commandments when they crucified Jesus. Do you think that it was a series of conditions wherein vengeance within the cosmos itself acted in an orderly manner? Is it in keeping with the philosophy "wickedness destroys the wicked" that it was rightly attributed to the weak relations of man to man?

Meditation: Even in despair may I cover moods of envy and despair with kindness and forgiveness! May I have influence in helping others so that they will not become bitter in calamity or weak for lack of faith! *Amen.*

October 16

PATIENCE IS A VIRTUE

"By your endurance you will gain your lives." (Luke 21:19)

Jesus could foresee calamity, but only the Father knew when it would come. In persecution as well as in times of joyful achievement the remnant of the early disciples remained steadfast. They expected that the day of glorification and restoration would come. Being glorified they would eat and drink at the table of the Lord and would turn many to a belief in the Gospel. They endured because they had hope of the resurrection, inasmuch as they had the Holy Spirit to guide and help them. They felt that like Jesus, they, too, should live.

Meditation: In these days of hurry and impatience let us be calm for we have the certainty that God is with us. May our hope and love turn people from evil ways into days of faithful service. To wait for You and work for You is not time lost. *Amen.*

October 17

THE UNPARDONABLE SIN

"Therefore, I tell you, every sin and blasphemy will be forgiven men, but the blasphemy against the Spirit will not be forgiven." (Matthew 12:31)

The divine justice was evidenced in healing the deaf and dumb man. The Pharisees analyzed this healing by saying that it was done by the prince of demons inasmuch as he only had the power to cast out demons. Jesus showed the fallacy of their argument on the grounds that if Satan or the prince of demons could cast out demons then Satan was inconsistent and showed division and weakness. In fairness the Pharisees should have admitted that the source of Jesus' power to cast out demons was the Spirit of God. Jesus took this opportunity to say that to reject or argue against the Spirit of God was blasphemy and that the constant rejection of the Spirit of

God was unforgiveable. This constant rejection of the Spirit of God and His righteousness to many is contrary to common sense and reason and is the unpardonable sin.

Meditation: The "Hound of Heaven" by Francis Thompson portrays the pursuit of the Spirit of God upon mankind. The Parable of the Prodigal Son (Luke 15:11-32) likewise demonstrates the constant concern and pursuit of us by the Gracious Heavenly Father. For Your constant concern, Our Father, we are thankful. *Amen.*

October 18

ILLIMITABLE FORGIVENESS

"Lord, how often shall my brother sin against me, and I forgive him? As many as seven times? Jesus said to him, I do not say to you seven times but seventy times seven." (Matthew 18:21)

Seventy times seven suggests illimitable forgiveness. One would not stop to count to such a high number each time he had forgiven or been forgiven. Jesus here turns the notion of unlimited revenge on the part of Lamech (Genesis 4:24) into unlimited forgiveness. The situation is reversed but the numbers are the same and this shows that the strong man is the forgiving man; whereas, in the days of Lamech and in the case of Lamech, himself, it was the pattern that the strong man was the cruel man, the unforgiving and the most revengeful man. Have you noted the change of thought that came through the centuries? Is this a confirmation that forgiveness is of God and the strongest element in human relations?

Meditation: Help me to forgive without limit! Let us thank God that we live in a land among people where we can receive, accept and abide by the communications of the Holy Spirit! *Amen.*

October 19
THE COMPASSION OF JESUS

"And a leper came to him, beseeching him . . . Moved with pity, he stretched out his hand . . . and said to him I will; be clean." (Mark 1:40-42)

The leper moved Jesus with compassion and the widow of Nain also moved Jesus with compassion. (Luke 7:13) In each case He responded by healing and restoring. The father of the Prodigal Son was moved with compassion when he saw the condition of his returning son. We are impressed with the fact that Jesus was moved with compassion when people came for help, whether they were prodigal, sick or sinful. Jesus was also disturbed when people substituted idols or inanimate gods for God Himself. The word translated compassion is the Greek word "splagchnizomai" which being further translated means "yearning in the region of the bowels." It suggests that compassion gives inward pain or hurt. Have you ever experienced the real pain of compassion in the heart or intestines?

Meditation: May we, like Jesus, know the real pain of compassion and like Him be able to do something about it. May we always remember that we also have power to help, to heal and to forgive! *Amen.*

October 20
THE SUBJECT OF MERCY

"And his mercy is on those who fear him from generation to generation." (Luke 1:50)

The idea of the mercy of God is definite and continuous. It conceives a continuous universe with continual need for mercy. This magnificat may have been one of the songs composed and sung by the early Christians and its summary of the goodness and concern of God is well done. God is a Saviour to the spirit of man, holy, merciful, strong, blessed, a

leader of Israel and also a dethroner of the tyrannical and unfaithful. The mercy that man shows comes through the mercy
and grace that God gives.

Meditation: "The mercy I to others show, that mercy show
to me.

For thy mercies, Lord, are sure, Thy compassion
doth endure."

last line from Hymn by
Greville Phillimore

October 21

THE MISSION OF JESUS

*"A light for revelation to the Gentiles and for glory to thy
people, Israel."* (Luke 2:32)

The Nunc Dimittis expresses satisfaction at the birth of
Jesus. To Simeon it marked the close of his own good life.
It may have been composed after the message and witness of
Jesus had been fully accepted by some of the Christians. The
revelation of God through Jesus was a world revelation. It
opened the doors of salvation to the Gentiles and, therefore,
brought glory to the people of Israel for through them had
come the knowledge of the intimacy of God. As the sun gives
light and warmth so the spirit of God gives light and warmth
to all. Is the Spirit of God being accepted and used by all
people? Why?

Meditation: May we, like Simeon, see the salvation which
God through Jesus had prepared. May we live many years to
help to realize the completeness of the work of our God!
Amen.

October 22
THE MESSAGE OF ZECHARIAH

*"To give knowledge of salvation to his people in the forgive-
ness of their sins, through the tender mercies of our God."*
(Luke 1:77-78a)

It is miraculous how the message of the Old Testament
shapes into the New. The universal scope of Jesus' mission
is shown in this message of Zechariah, the message of the
angels, the magnificat, etc. The birth of Jesus and the early
descriptions of new revelations and inspirations reminds one
of Jacob's ladder where angels ascend and descend, as they
carry messages back and forth, convincing man that God is
concerned and present. Both tell us that heaven and earth
are not so far apart that they cannot be connected with a
ladder, even if it is only a ladder of prayer.

Meditation: We are grateful that the incarnation is real and
the word Emmanuel is evidence that "God is with us." May
the song of the angels become an Eternal song and message
for all who like to give and receive good will! *Amen.*

October 23
LIGHT ON THE PROBLEM OF DEATH

*"The people who sat in darkness have seen a great light, and
for those who sat in the region of the shadow of death light
has dawned."* (Matthew 4:16)

People in spiritual darkness had a new insight as a result
of Jesus' life and His teaching, crucifixion and resurrection.
The aweful shadow of death disappeared. The resurrection
gave death a new meaning. We have shown that vengeance
among persons brings harm. Even attempts to do wrong add
to the wrong. We have learned that forgiveness of man to
man brings reconciliation. Even an effort to forgive a wrong
brings new meaning to the one who seeks forgiveness. Vengeance of God becomes the Judgment of God, the Supreme

Judge, and philosophically speaking it is within the cosmos or universe itself. We have learned that wickedness tends to destroy and separate but that righteousness rewards and builds.

Meditation: Help us to overcome and give no quarter to habits that tend to enslave and destroy us! Save us from habits that harm! *Amen.*

October 24

THE GOLDEN RULE

"So whatever you wish that men would do to you, do so to them; for this is the law and the prophets." (Matthew 7:12)

We have now reached the summum bonum of moral insight and practice. The Golden Rule links God with man in relation to each other among all people. The negative form of the Golden Rule is given in Tobit 4:16, and both its positive and negative forms are expressed in the Bible. It was the genius of Jesus to set it forth in positive, clear form. Please note that Jesus made it a summation of all teachings and implications of the law and the prophets. Here we have a statement of the principle of love in action. Judgment must enter into each decision. Reason should be used before each action or decision. It may become automatic in its application. It is not possession or submission but a corrective moral force. Is Religion friendship? Horace Bushnell thought it was "friendship with God and men."

Meditation: May the Golden Rule continue to be golden for me! May I be worthy of the worth it contains! Keep alive in me the spark of celestial fire and warmth called conscience! *Amen.*

October 25

LOVE YOUR ENEMIES

"Love your enemies, do good to those who hate you, bless those who curse you, pray for those who abuse you." (Luke 6:27b-28)

Love is the norm of the Golden Rule. Respect for the situation of others is primary in our fellowship as Christians. The Greek word for "love" is "Agape" which minimizes "love" as possession. It is both subjective and objective. Love is in one person or God as subject and another person or God as object. Love is personal. We love God and persons. We like flowers and things. The basis of love in action is the reaching forth of the SELF toward God or another person. The SELF reaching forth is the subject and the SELF reached is the object. Therefore in Christian fellowship we reach forth to help an enemy with the hope that the enemy will reach forth to help us. Subjectively we hope to change the attitude of an enemy to that of the attitude of a friend.

Meditation: Help me to have self-control in speaking or dealing with one who is unfriendly. May we have faith to believe that we can turn or change an enemy into a friend remembering that You, God, are the intervening Friend. *Amen.*

October 26

THE GREAT COMMANDMENT

"You shall love the Lord your God with all your heart, and with all your soul, and with all your mind. This is the great and first commandment. And a second is like it, You shall love your neighbor as yourself." (Matthew 22:37-39) (cf. Mark 12:28-32)

The answer to the lawyer is conclusive. It is the Shema that begins "Hear, O Israel," and emphasizes the love of God (Deuteronomy 6:4) which, united to the phrase in Leviticus 19:18, brings mankind as an object of love in all dealings.

With righteousness as the aim or target—seek first the kingdom of God and his righteousness (Matthew 6:33)—and love as the method. We have a form of fellowship that is in keeping with the Golden Rule.

Meditation: "Stoop to my weakness, mighty as thou art
And make me love thee as I ought to love."
lines from Hymn of George Croly

October 27
MATHEMATICS AND LOGIC

"For this is the law and the prophets." (Matthew 7:12)
"On these two commandments depend all the law and the prophets." (Matthew 22:40)

The Golden Rule (Matthew 7:12) and the two Great Commandments (Matthew 37-39) are supported by the phrase "the law and the prophets," which must mean that the Golden Rule and the Great Commandments comprehend in meaning all the "law and the prophets" as we have them in the Old Testament. If they both summarize the law and the prophets then they are equal to each other and the Golden Rule equals the Great Commandments or the Rule of Love. The genius of Jesus was the combining of these two similar and comprehensive truths.

Meditation: Our Father, in studying the Old and New Testaments we see the stream of compassion, confrontation, care and forgiveness reaching a climax in the Trinity of Love which includes love to God, the love of God to man, the love of man to man and the love or respect for the SELF or person himself. *Amen.*

October 28
LOVE AND PERSONALITY

"Hear, O Israel: the Lord our God, the Lord is one: and you shall love the Lord your God with all your heart, and

with all your soul, and with all your mind and with all your strength." (Mark 12:29-30)

The scribe asked Jesus: What commandment is first of all? (Mark 12:28) The first lawyer asked: What is the great commandment in the law? (Matthew 22:36) The second lawyer asked: What shall I do to inherit eternal life? (Luke 10:25) The order, variant uses and versions are interesting and are as follows:

Hebrew

heart	soul		might	Deuteronomy 6:5

Septuagint (Greek)

mind	soul		strength	Deuteronomy 6:5

Jesus

heart	soul	mind	strength	Mark 12:30

Scribe

heart	understanding		strength	Mark 12:33

Jesus to First Lawyer

heart	soul		mind	Matthew 22:37

Jesus to Second Lawyer

heart	soul	strength	mind	Luke 10:27

In the six uses no two have the same order:

5 have heart
5 have soul
4 have mind
4 have strength
1 has might
1 has understanding

Meditation: All agree on the need for love to God as a part of the Great Commandment and the Shema. We are grateful for this synthesis of the need of personal love and assurance which all six uses show concerning love. Help me to love You more and more. *Amen.*

October 29

LOVE AND THE SELF

"You shall love your neighbor as yourself." (Matthew 22:39)
"You shall love . . . your neighbor as yourself." (Luke 10:27)
"You shall love your neighbor as yourself." (Mark 12:31)
"You shall love your neighbor as yourself." (Leviticus 19:18)
"You shall love your neighbor as yourself." (Matthew 19:19)
"You shall love your neighbor as yourself." (Romans 13:9)

The last two are connected with Old Testament Commandments and strangely enough they are the Ten Commandments. This suggests the importance attached to it. The lawyer asked Jesus, "Who is My neighbor?" Jesus gave him the Parable of the Good Samaritan which seemed to show that a neighbor is not confined to location, sect, relationship, tribe or caste. Do you think the lawyer accepted the sociological implications? Can we think of a neighbor in the philosophical or the psychological or the religious sense? Are you a neighbor?

Meditation: Now that distance has been shortened by travel time, our national neighbors have become closer and more numerous. Shall we pray that neighbors may accept and appreciate neighborliness? *Amen.*

October 30

JUSTIFICATION OF THE SELF

"But he, desiring to justify himself said: And who is my neighbor?" (Luke 10:29)

The lawyer knew the commandments. He evidently felt embarrassed when the law of love was defined and tried to justify himself by asking about the scope of neighborliness. Jesus defined it in terms of need rather than community, race or sect. Jesus made a Samaritan a neighbor. The lawyer must have felt condemned rather than justified. What do you think was the mental reaction of the lawyer to Jesus' definition of a neighbor?

Meditation: We thank You that mercy drops as the gentle dew of heaven and that it blesses the one who gives and the one who receives. Shakespeare was right in thinking of it as an attribute of God Himself. *Amen.*

October 31
FORGIVENESS AND DEVOTION

"I tell you, her sins, which are many are forgiven. For she loved much but he who is forgiven little, loves little." (Luke 7:47)

The dialogue of Jesus and Simon helps us to understand how one should and can love his neighbor as himself. The woman in Simon's house washed the feet of Jesus, wiped them with tears and anointed them with ointment and kissed them. This act of devotion was beyond anything Simon had done. Both Jesus and Simon seemed to agree that there were degrees of love and degrees of forgiveness. There seemed to be no limit to forgiveness. A determined desire for forgiveness may induce a person to do unusual acts to atone for the wrong. The woman's devotion and forgiveness had witnesses and this may have been a manifestation of her sincerity and need for forgiveness. Do you believe that complete forgiveness is possible?

Meditation: Forgive us our sins as we forgive those who sin against us. May peace follow forgiveness! *Amen.*

November 1
LOVE AND FAITH

"Your faith has saved you: go in peace." (Luke 7:50b)

When Simon was critical Jesus began to appeal to his inner sense regarding hospitality. Simon seems to have held Jesus at a distance compared to the devotion of the woman. Her appreciation of Jesus' teaching, compassion and inner power made her sense her own need for forgiveness and she did not want the opportunity of Jesus' presence to be lost. What Simon seemed to think foolish proved to be the Gospel in action. The faith of the woman was her salvation. Peace had replaced guilt in her soul and mind and the forgiveness, which was much, was complete. She seemed to have received more of the spirit of God in the presence of Jesus than Simon did. Is it ever wise to do the unusual to remove guilt?

Meditation: May faith give adventure, adventure healing, forgiveness righteousness and righteousness love! *Amen.*

November 2

THE REAL SELF

"But when he came to himself." (Luke 15:17a)

The son when a prodigal was not himself. Was it the assertiveness of the submerged or unconscious self that made him a prodigal? Was it the id? May it have been an envious effort to escape restraint? After being a fugitive from God and his parents he became lonely, dependent, poor, uncomfortable and forsaken. The secondary self had failed him and the real SELF began to assert itself. He concluded that he had sinned. The lack of faith in the unreal self had become complete. With the real self in control he decided to return home where the real ties were restored and forgiveness was completed. The real self finds its complement with and in the Father. He was pursued by his father's spirit and concern as zealously as a hound pursues its quarry. Have we learned that we are constantly confronted by the compassionate spirit of God? Is it ever wise to substitute the companionship of men for the companionship of God?

Meditation: We are thankful that the Parable of the Gracious Father emphasizes the importance of the SELF. When we submit to the weaker elements of our personality we are already lost. When we discover we are lost we should quickly return. *Amen.*

November 3
THE PARENTHOOD OF GOD

"How often would I have gathered your children together as a hen gathers her brood under her wings and you would not." (Matthew 23:37b)

It was a sad day for Jesus when he wept over Jerusalem. He had tried to help the people but they would not respond. Did they think they were self-sufficient? His concern for the people stemmed from His compassion. The compassion of Jesus had been shown at the feeding of the five thousand, when He restored the sight to the blind, when He blessed the children and when He had restored the son of the widow of Nain. These elements of compassion in Jesus showed his compassion and concern. Why did the people of Jerusalem not respond to a man of sorrows and become acquainted with grief?

Meditation: Help us to help people to sense their real needs! *Amen.*

November 4
PERSISTENT PRAYER PREVAILS

"Vindicate me against my adversary." (Luke 18:3)

The widow seems to have been tormented by an adversary. Legal minded people seemed to be inclined to take advantage of orphans and widows. For a time the judge did not pay much attention, but her persistence induced him to review the case and give judgment in her favor. Was Jesus teaching that God was judge and that if we will continue in prayer and have concern for justice and righteousness we may find release from whatever adversary is bothering us? In each of us there may be a spiritual asset that no adversary can spoil or steal. Does Jesus here show that if an earthly judge will respond to a persistent concern then much more will the judge, the righteous Judge, hear and respond to us?

Meditation: Here we find the effectual value of prayer without ceasing! May we pray aright, for if we pray aright we will think right and do right. The incentive to do right is stronger than the desire to do evil. *Amen.*

November 5
THE PRAYER OF THE PUBLICAN

"God be merciful to me a sinner." (Luke 18:13d)

Repentance, humility, devotion and worship undergird the prayer of this publican. What he asked for himself he wished for others also. The prayer of the Pharisee showed pride, self-sufficiency, intolerance and probably bigotry and self-glorification. He compared himself with others when he should have compared himself with God. The publican glorified God and in Jesus' opinion he, himself, was glorified. The Pharisees glorified themselves and history teaches that they were abased. Notice the courage of Jesus in giving this parable about the Pharisee when Pharisees may have been present.

Meditation: Humble us so we may glorify You. We are grateful for Your grace and favor and we want to have a great measure of Your Spirit! *Amen.*

November 6
WHO IS WITHOUT SIN

"And again he stepped down, and wrote on the ground." (John 8:8 A.V.)

"And once more he bent down and wrote with his finger on the ground." (John 8:8 footnote in R.S.V.)

This incident is more in keeping with the synoptic Gospels than with John. The enormity of the sin was not in question. The interpretation of the law and the execution thereof was the problem. Jesus did not condone the sin or presume to sit in judicial judgment. Jerome and other commentators think that He may have written the names of sins of which the by-standers may have been guilty. As the names of various sins were before them on the ground He called upon anyone without sin to cast the first stone. The disappearance of the accusers indicated guilt and each one felt condemned for his own sin and this led them to do nothing. The words of Jesus "sin no more" may well serve as good advice to all. Is this an instance when Jesus by His superior wisdom saved a life? Notice that each of the accusers became a judge of himself and each gave sentence to himself.

Meditation: We know that if we sin we have an advocate with the Father. If we have sinned let us sin no more. May the Presence of God in us keep us steadfast! *Amen.*

November 7

WHAT IS GOD

"God is Spirit." (John 4:24a)

In the beginning of our study we learned that God was Spirit (Genesis 1:2). The woman of Sychar evidently did not think of Him in that manner. Persons now have difficulty in thinking of God as Spirit. When Jesus had explained the nature of God as Spirit, she associated Jesus with Messiahship and later regarded Jesus as a Saviour. Today we may not understand all that involves God as Spirit but we do know enough about the Spirit of God to have a good spirit in ourselves. The Holy Spirit of God may be the greatest power of the universe. Can you fully understand electricity? Can you touch a current of electricity or feel only the effect of that current? Can you touch the person of the Holy Spirit or only sense the effects?

Meditation: May the Holy Spirit pervade my own spirit and control it. *Amen.*

November 8
THE LOVE OF THE FATHER

"For this reason the Father loves men, because I lay down my life that I may take it again." (John 10:17)

Having described Himself as the Good Shepherd He characterized Himself as laying down His life for the sheep. The people were His concern as sheep are the concern of the shepherd. He would sacrifice His life on the cross in the faith that His mission would be approved of God. Through the faithfulness of Jesus the power of God would restore Him to the disciples and they would accept Him forever as the Good Shepherd. Is it true that love will give life itself for the purpose of helping and saving others? Can love be shown in a better way than by giving it freely in service?

Meditation: We are grateful for the message of the Good Shepherd and that Jesus regards us as members of His flock. May we never stray and cause concern and anxiety! *Amen.*

November 9
UNANIMITY WITH GOD

"I and the Father are one." (John 10:30)

God was His Father and He was God's Son. Their interests were the same. The saving needs among men were the same. The power to heal was similar and the Spirit in each was the same. It was, therefore, easy for Jesus to think of Himself as one with the Father. He felt that His mission was to do the Father's will and to proclaim the way of righteousness through the method of love. The words on the cross, "today, thou shalt be with me in Paradise," show that the power and judgment of Jesus as to the future did not differentiate between Himself and the Father. He was the human revealer of the Divine and, therefore, was Himself Divine.

Meditation: May we also be at one with God. Make every

day be a day of atonement for me! Help me to start each day clean. *Amen.*

November 10

THE ORDER OF NATURE

"Unless a grain of wheat falls into the earth and dies, it remains alone; but if it dies, it bears much fruit." (John 12:24)

One must sow to reap. Grain must disintegrate to become a living stock or plant. Corn must be assimilated with the soil and change its form if it will produce other corn. The outer husk must disintegrate. Jesus understood nature and integrated His own life with it. We need to integrate our living spirit with the living Spirit of God. Jesus was familiar with nature. As the nature we know changes in its persistence to live it evidences our own immortality. Do you study nature to know the Spirit?

Meditation: "Lord, obediently we go, Gladly leaving all **below;**

Only Thou our leader be, And we still will follow Thee."

lines from Hymn by John Cennick

November 11

A NEW COMMANDMENT

"A new commandment I give to you, that you love one another, even as I have loved you." (John 13:34)

This commandment stems, like the Great Commandment, from the two commandments of love in the Old Testament. (Deuteronomy 6:4; Leviticus 19:18) It is given when Jesus was speaking intimately with His disciples. It is brief but comprehensive. It suggests the depth of His love as active among the disciples. It is subjective in that the Self love of Jesus reached forth to them as objects. Is real love the giving of oneself to help the loved?

Meditation: We believe this commandment came from the heart of Jesus. It is positive, on-going and inspires us to thought as well as action. May Your love have uniting power for all mankind! Help me to love as God loves! *Amen.*

November 12
THE TEST OF DISCIPLESHIP

"By this all men will know that you are my disciples, if you have love for one another." (John 13:35)

Jesus makes love the test of discipleship. Jesus does not make a belief or creed the test, although these may help in compassing love. The test of discipleship is a life lived with love as the motivating method of action. Jesus does not give any conditions. It is unvarnished love for one another that is the test. It is each person working to develop another personality. In helping another to be Godlike one may become Godlike himself. (cf. Matthew 25:42-44) Do we deny Christ when we make an organization or a person a substitute for Jesus' statement of the test of discipleship? Should churches make "love for one another" the test of discipleship?

Meditation: May the test of discipleship be applied to me now. May my real SELF and my unconscious self testify to the power and value of Christian love! *Amen.*

November 13
LOVE KEEPS THE COMMANDMENTS

"If you keep my commandments, you will abide in my love." (John 15:10)

The word, commandments, is in the plural. He must have included the Great Commandments as well as other commandments that emphasized the need and understanding of Christian love. Love becomes a steadying factor in keeping the commandments. The Ten Commandments have never been abrogated. To keep the commandments makes love positive, active and alive. It reaches into every form of life, including the social, religious, economic, moral, mental, psychological, spiritual, philosophical and physical.

Meditation: Help me to keep the commandments. They substantiate my beliefs. They challenge my intelligence and the keeping of them makes the spirit of love grow. *Amen.*

November 14
JESUS KEPT THE COMMANDMENTS

"I have kept my Father's commandments and abide in his love." (John 15:10b)

The power of the commandments in keeping love alive had been tested by Jesus. His advice to the disciples then and now was not a "fly by night" proposition. The close of His earthly life testified that love had been proved. The keeping of the commandments unites oneself with others who keep the commandments so that individual love for God becomes collective love in an accumulative manner. The fact that Jesus lived the life of love and declared Himself victorious and was pronounced victorious through the resurrection and the Holy Spirit should bring joy. This positive joy He declared to his disciples when He told them the method by which their "joy should be made full." (John 15:11c) Will the spirit of love in action among mankind kill the germs of war and hate?

Meditation: Make my love for You and mankind be the supreme motive of my life. May Your love come to me, be nourished in me and conveyed through me to others! *Amen.*

November 15
THE GREATER LOVE

"Greater love has no man than this, that a man lay down his life for his friends. You are my friends if you do what I command you." (John 15:13-14)

We have had this thought before in connection with the

parable of the Good Shepherd. (John 10:1-17) Jesus is here talking with and to His disciples and it is no parable. It is an injunction and statement. He assures them that His love is given to the nth degree. To love God and to give the message of God was His mission even if He had to forfeit His earthly life in doing it. As the Great Commandments are the summation of the way of love so the giving of His life on the cross is the summation of the highest offering of all offerings.

Meditation: May the love of Jesus be in me. May the love of Jesus in me make and keep many friends. If we are friends of one another we automatically become friends of Jesus! *Amen.*

November 16
THE PROMISE OF THE COMFORTER

"When the Counselor comes whom I shall send to you from the Father, even the Spirit of truth, who proceeds from the Father, he will bear witness to me; and you also are witnesses, because you have been with me from the beginning." (John 15:26-27)

Jesus left nothing undone. He thought of the disciples and prepared them to receive the Holy Spirit after He had gone. The Comforter or Counselor is the Holy Spirit. It is the power of God that enters into the mind or spirit of man with His quickening love and helps in every righteous act or deed. The Father is the source of the Holy Spirit, and a witness to the power and love of God to work righteousness. This Spirit should be a witness and the disciples should witness since they had been with him from the beginning. To witness to the power of God through Christ was to be their mission. Did they live up to their mission? Does the Holy Spirit embody the trinity of love which is love to God, love of God to man and the love of man to man?

Meditation: May the Holy Spirit favor us. May the grace of

God sustain us and the Holy Spirit inspire us to accept and keep the way of love! *Amen.*

November 17
UNANIMITY OF DISCIPLESHIP

"That they may be one even as we are one, I in them and thou in me, that they may become perfectly one." (John 17:22b-23a)

Jesus said that the Father had given Him His glory and Jesus wanted the disciples to share this glory so that the binding power of God's love would keep them together. The parting message was filled with the assurance that through the Holy Spirit they would be bound together with one purpose, aim and mission. The binding force seems to have been the Holy Spirit.

Meditation: "Come Holy Spirit, heavenly Dove, With all thy quickening powers;

Come, shed abroad a Saviour's love, And that shall kindle ours."

stanza from hymn by Isaac Watts

November 18
THE LAST SUPPER

"I have earnestly desired to eat this passover with you before I suffer." (Luke 22:15)

The Passover was the annual occasion among the Jewish people when the care of God for them was dramatized with a specially prepared meal. It recalled how the older sons of the Egyptians were struck down while the sons of the Hebrews were spared. It was a family gathering and still is a family occasion when God's care is memorialized. Jesus wanted to observe this supper with His disciples for He evidently felt that they had family interests and concerns. Was His suffering on the cross to be for love's sake? Did He want to go the limit of sacrifice that He might teach them how God's love reaches down to lift people up? He accepted no favors, wielded no physical power, used no means of self-defense to mar His self-sacrificing mission. In the passing of the bread and cup at the close of the Passover meal He went further than usual and told of the New Covenant sealed with His blood.

Meditation: "Thy body broken for my sake, My bread from
                    heav'n shall be;
             Thy testamental cup I take, And thus remember
             thee." *Amen.*

                                                        Anonymous

November 19

IN THE GARDEN

"Let this cup pass from me, nevertheless, not as I will, but as thou wilt." (Matthew 26:39)

These words in the garden express a unity with the Father in doing His will. The ordeal of the cross was near. Jesus had previously taught that He and the Father were One and He continued to make the will of God of primary importance. Was this prayer a request that His faith in the love of God would not fail? Jesus left to God what His will should be. After the resurrection the disciples thought the will of God had been done, the Scripture was fulfilled and the love of God for all men was vindicated. The present day disciples remember Jesus now by the real or symbolic bread of his broken body, and the cup as the real or symbol of his shed blood in what is called communion by some, the Lord's supper by others and the Mass or Eucharist by still others.

Meditation: May my love for You be unbroken, eternal and genuine. *Amen.*

November 20

HE SAVED OTHERS

"He saved others; he cannot save himself." (Matthew 27:42a)

This taunt fitted into the philosophy and the nature of the religion of those ridiculing Jesus while He was on the cross. To save oneself physically was in keeping with the law of self-preservation. Jesus, however, attached more importance to the saving of the soul—the life we have with God. Jesus trusted in spiritual force. In a sense the taunt—He saved others—was true but it was not true that spiritually He did not save Himself. The crowd rated the saving of oneself from the cross as primary, whereas Jesus regarded the saving of the soul and the vindication of the power of righteousness and love as primary. The philosophy of Jesus was "I go away but I will come again to you" (John 14:28), which shows the ultimate victory of the spirit. In saving others He saved Himself and the world.

Meditation: In the dark and weariness of life we may be sorely tried but I have faith with Emily Dickinson who said, "If my bark sink 'tis another sea. Mortality's ground floor is immortality." *Amen.*

November 21

FORGIVENESS TO THE UTTERMOST

"Father forgive them; for they know not what they do." (Luke 23:34a)

These words show complete mastery of Himself. He blessed those who had despitefully used and persecuted Him as He had taught His disciples to do. He relied on the purity of His own heart. It was turning the other cheek. It was blessing those who cursed. It was showing mercy for cruelty. It was forgiving without limit and universal in its scope.

Meditation: Our Father, we are convinced that spiritual

power is greater than physical force. May the proof of the immortality that was in Jesus extend to us! May I be worthy of immortality! *Amen.*

November 22
COMMITTED HIMSELF TO GOD

"Father, into thy hands I commit my spirit." (Luke 23:46b)

Jesus on the cross had complete control. His spirit came from God and was committed to God in life and forever. Whatever the situation He was safe in the hands of God. The assurance Jesus gave the thief and the forgiveness to those who crucified Him manifest control and power almost beyond the imagination. The way of love had not failed. The judgment of God is kindly judgment to those who do His will. As Jesus had commended Himself to do God's will it was only natural that in His extremity He should again commit Himself to God. What do you think of Jesus' future? Is He now at the right hand of God?

Meditation: As the women, with others, laid His body in the tomb, it was with haste for they wanted to keep the religious law in regard to the keeping of the sabbath. Their concern for Jesus was also for themselves. The care of Jesus' body manifested love at work. *Amen.*

November 23
THE LOVE OF THE DISCIPLE

"Lord, you know everything; you know that I love you." (John 21:17f)

The resurrection came the third day after the crucifixion. Victory followed the cross. The witness of the disciples was vocal, definite and undeniable. The fact that He asked for complete love shows one purpose of His mission. If love was complete then the care for the disciples would assure the success of His death on the cross. Part time love would not be sufficient. Complete dedication was necessary. The disciples gave the assurance that Jesus wanted. History reveals that they worked with a definite commitment and dedication to the love of God as it was manifested in Him Who had become their Saviour. What is the greatest saying of Jesus in your opinion?

Meditation: May my witness be as definite and convincing as that of the early disciples. May the love of God be the foundation principle of every disciple now and forever! *Amen.*

November 24
FULFILLMENT OF THE OLD TESTAMENT

"As a nursing father bare he them in the wilderness." (Acts 13:18 American Rev., see Deuteronomy 1:31)
"He bore with them in the wilderness." (Acts 13:18)

The journey through the wilderness from Egypt to Canaan gave the people of Israel assurance as to the care of God. As a father holds his child in his strong arms so God helped and protected Israel. The care had continued through the centuries. Luke, the author of the Acts, portrays the hard times of persecution which the disciples endured in their devotion to what they thought were the teachings of Jesus. He shows God at work by historical references. The message of the living Lord and the certainty of His presence steeled them to speak what they believed came from God. They felt they were disciples and had a mission. Are we as faithful in our discipleship as the early disciples?

Meditation: We glory in the book of the Acts because it shows how the early disciples gloried in the Lord. The examples of courage, faith, hope and love gave witness to the reality of the resurrection, the fulfillment of the Scriptures and the righteousness of God. *Amen.*

November 25
FULFILLMENT OF THE LAW

"For the whole law is fulfilled in one word, 'You shall love your neighbor as yourself.' " (Galatians 5:14)

Paul accepted the grace of God which made him and others to be sons of God. The Golden Rule and the Shema, with complete love to God and the command to love the neighbor as the self, were taught by Paul and thought to be a summation of the law and the prophets. Here Paul makes love for a neighbor the complete fulfillment of the law; for Paul, being brought up with the law, tried to fulfill it but he could do it only as a Christian. The spiritual law is based on judgment, intelligence, emotion, love and good will.

Meditation: We are thankful that we can keep the covenant with freedom in our favor and love our supporting power. *Amen.*

November 26
HELPING ONE ANOTHER

"Bear one another's burdens, and so fulfill the law of Christ." (Galatians 6:2)

Paul not only stated the spiritual law but gave practical interpretations of the law of love in action. If religion is based on the power of love as workable, then Paul is practical and gives courage and praise to those who effect it. To help others is human and to work with them in bearing their burdens is only natural. It justifies one's faith in the effectiveness of love. Faith is love at work. To bear one another's burdens shows the strength of love.

Meditation: May we continue to have faith that helpfulness toward another gives the greatest satisfactions. May the way of helpfulness become automatic in me. *Amen.*

November 27
THE FRUIT OF THE SPIRIT

"The fruit of the Spirit is love, joy, peace, patience, kindness, goodness, faithfulness, gentleness, self-control; against such there is no law." (Galatians 5:23)

It was true that against this there was no law in Paul's day and we should rejoice that there is no law against being righteous and securing spiritual yield now. The above spiritual elements are sought to effect good will wherever they prevail. If the above fruits of the spirit are achieved through Christian love, the lusts of the flesh will be overcome or smothered by good deeds and holy thoughts supported by worship. How complete are the fruits of the Spirit as given by Paul? Can you name others?

Meditation: When we live and walk with a desire to help another person, through our personality, we make the Christian spirit in us radiate itself to others. *Amen.*

November 28
LOVE IS TAUGHT OF GOD

"You, yourselves, have been taught by God to love one another." (1 Thessalonians 4:9b)

Love is taught of God, Paul thinks. Does he mean that it is inherent in each person? Who does not exult at the smile of a child? Have you noticed how well a child responds with love to the love of a parent? If love is inherent, then the conduct of Christians should of itself induce them not to destroy one another or to defraud one another but to live and work with brotherly love. He seems to conclude that one inherently loves and does the things that proper love should do and that this method of action should be encouraged and universalized. Have you experienced brotherly love in any organization of which you are a part? Should love for parents toward their children be deep?

Meditation: While we are under the law of love we are also justified through its operation, and if we live by the law of love the need for subsidiary laws will be minimized. *Amen.*

November 29
RULES OF CONDUCT

"See that none of you repays evil for evil, but always seek to do good to one another and to all." (1 Thessalonians 5:15)

Having lived under the laws of the Pharisees and also under the law of love, Paul had come to the conclusion that the law of revenge had been completely abrogated and nullified through the life and death of Christ. In place of the law of revenge it was that of love. To him love was universal. Does the law of love work effectively for you?

Meditation: We rejoice because we were born and live in a land where the law of love may be worked without restraint or fear. We thank You that love has been proved efficient, whereas the law of revenge has been proved to be destructive. *Amen.*

November 30
ABOUND IN LOVE

"And may the Lord make you increase and abound in love to one another and to all men, as we do to you." (1 Thessalonians 3:12)

This verse gives a splendid description of the SELF in its operation toward other selves. As he prays that the Thessalonians may increase and abound in love he thought of himself and the other Christians in their relations to the Thessalonians and added "even as we do to you." He is here asking them to do only what they would like to have others do if they were in their place. It is a good practical example of the Golden Rule in action. Do you like to think that the Golden

Rule, the law of love and the fulfilling of the law mean the same sort of conduct?
Meditation: We thank You for the embodiment of love in Your Son. May we, like Him, abound in love, be grounded in love and may it become a norm in being tactful and helpful to others. *Amen.*

December 1
LOVE EDIFIES

"Knowledge puffs up, but love builds up." (1 Corinthians 8:1)

Paul's practical advice was sought by the Corinthians as well as by the Galatians and Thessalonians. He told the Corinthians that there was a difference between knowledge and love. Questions about eating meat, circumcision, sacrificing to idols and eating meat sacrificed to idols, disorder at the Lord's table, etc., were to be decided by the manner in which they edified the worshipper. Did each man have a conscience and an influence and, if eating meat sacrificed to idols caused another to question his loyalty and devotion, then would he sacrifice by not eating any meat? For the sake of a weak brother it is well to abstain. Should one abstain from alcoholic beverages, tobacco, etc., for the sake of its possible harm to others? Paul said abstain. What do you say?
Meditation: Help us to abstain from doing what may influence others to be harmed by weakening their faith or self-control. *Amen.*

December 2
DO THINGS IN LOVE

"Let all that you do be done in love." (1 Corinthians 16:14)

This is an unqualified statement. Love is the norm of action and it often requires strength as well as faith to keep it active. Regardless of situations, Christians should let love be the predominating factor in judgment and in decisions. Even if others do not employ the law of love and misinterpret your spirit and literally place you on the cross we must remember that the cross exemplified the power of love and that it led beyond the cross itself into the resurrection. Beyond the cross there may always be a crown and the crown may be one of victory and immortality. Can all things be done in love?

Meditation: May life bring its joys in spite of its problems. May we make disappointments become blessings, temptations a crown of righteousness and the cross a resurrection! *Amen.*

December 3

THE HYMN OF LOVE

"Love never ends." (1 Corinthians 8:1a)
"Faith, hope and love, these three but the greatest of these is love." (1 Corinthians 13:13)

Read the thirteenth chapter of first Corinthians, which is sometimes called The Hymn of Love. It is one of the best descriptions of love in all literature. It describes love as positive, firm, enduring, believing, hopeful and being able to adjust to changes in relation to the age of a person. It places love as more commendatory than hate, revenge, jealousy, suspicion and other negative elements. I know of no great positive hymn of hate. Love is not limited to races, time, colonies, places or nations. Love is an inherent gift. It should be kept pure, clean and holy. Do you think this Hymn of Love was sung by the early Christians? Will someone put it into a musical setting for use in our churches? Will someone create an oratorio using the words of this Hymn?

Meditation: We are grateful for this early hymn. May we read it, memorize it, recite it and live in its teachings! *Amen.*

December 4

FOLLOW AFTER LOVE

"Make love your aim, and earnestly desire the spiritual gifts."
(1 Corinthians 14:1a)

The thirteenth chapter of first Corinthians portrays love as strong, vital, constant and worthy of fulfillment in the home, church, nation and social groups. Love is a foundation for philosophy, sociology, psychology and religion. Jesus was the embodiment of love and each phase and phrase of the description of love was fulfilled in him. The first letter to the Corinthians closes with the words " let all that you do be done in love." (1 Corinthians 16:14) Note that there are no conditions in the description of love. Are there misunderstandings about love? Do some people associate it with the emotions only?

Meditation: I promise to make pure love my aim beginning with my family. May we never doubt the power of love and always remember that it is a positive force. *Amen.*

December 5

THE LOVE OF CHRIST

"For the love of Christ controls us, because we are convinced that one had died for all . . . that those who live might live no longer for themselves, but for Him who for their sake died and was raised." (2 Corinthians 5:14ab-15bd)

Here we have Paul giving a meaning of the death of Christ. His death was for a purpose. The resurrection completed that purpose and should control and challenge us to live the life of love. We can become new creatures when we become reconciled to God through Christ. If we are dissatisfied with ourselves let us let Christ take us over and His Spirit control us. If we cannot control ourselves we should have intelligence enough to let Christ do it. We should never surrender to evil? Because of controlling love in us we are ambassadors of Christ to reconcile the world to God.

Meditation: Having been reconciled to God through Christ, we want Your Spirit to help us in helping others to become reconciled to God through the gateway of love. *Amen.*

December 6
REVENGE BECOMES A LIABILITY

"Repay no one evil for evil, but take thought for what is noble in the sight of all." (Romans 12:17)

"Never avenge yourselves, but leave it to the wrath of God; for it is written 'Vengeance is mine' I will repay, says the Lord." (Romans 12:19)

Paul evidently had thought through the values and disvalues of life and had evidently come to the conclusion that love had the highest value and that revenge was a debit. The rule of love cancels the law of revenge so that if love rules there is no place for revenge. Love is supreme. Christians should resign themselves to God Who is the Justifier. Vengeance is a matter for God the Creator Who will recompense according to justice. God's universal plan is supreme. God's knowledge is unlimited and, therefore, God's method of dealing with injustice is beyond the knowledge of man. The primitive law of revenge was proved to be defective. What was the purpose of revenge? Was it to get justice by doing equal or greater harm to the one who had harmed?

Meditation: Since we have lived beyond the period of time when it was regarded as man's duty to revenge, it is no wonder that fear of harm is inherent in so many persons. May each of us have sufficient faith in love so that we can cast out fear! *Amen.*

December 7
LOVE IS A PRINCIPLE OF ACTION

"If your enemy is hungry, feed him; if he is thirsty, give him to drink; for by so doing you will heap burning coals upon his head." (Romans 12:20)

This quotation from Proverbs (Proverbs 25:21-22) is a proper Christian method to deal with an enemy. It is rendering good for evil. The implication is that the enemy is expecting evil treatment in return for the evil he has done. Instead he has received kindness, including food and drink. With shame in his mind and in his subconscience self he becomes uncomfortable, blushes with redness and his temperature rises as if coals of fire were on his head. What a superb figure! Have you heard of people whose blood pressure rises when they are ashamed or guilty?

Meditation: Help us to observe that this Scripture is in keeping with the Great Commandments, the Golden Rule, the Rule of Love and the teachings of Jesus. *Amen.*

December 8
THE FULFILLING OF THE LAW

"Owe no man anything, except to love one another; for he who loves his neighbor has fulfilled the law." (Romans 13:8)
"You shall not covet and any other commandment, are summed up in this sentence, 'You shall love your neighbor as yourself.' Loves does no wrong to a neighbor; therefore love is the fulfilling of the law." (Romans 13:9fg, 10)

These series of statements substantiate the effectiveness of love in practice. Love is defined as *fulfilling* the *law,* and it helps to keep the Ten Commandments, the Golden Rule, the Great Commandments, etc. Love released Paul from mental bondage. He once was a legalist but through the understanding of the love of God he became spiritually free. He had

Christ as his authority and through him he was bound to the universe, knowing that "each one of us shall give account of himself to God." (Romans 14:12) Each person including Paul, himself, was under the law of God through Christ.
Meditation: Help us to extend our own idea of neighborliness! May our neighbors be edified through us! *Amen.*

December 9
THE INNER SENSE

"Let each of us please his neighbor for his good, to edify him." (Romans 15:2)
"For Chirst did not please himself; but as it is written 'the reproaches of those who reproached thee fell on me.'" (Psalm 69:9) (Romans 15:3)

Each man may have an inner sense which is better than himself. This is the true or inner self. Life becomes free and victorious when the inner sense enriches life and helps to weld all people together in righteousness through love. Our ability to project the love of God through the SELF into others is the ultimate test of life. We see the person as an object but the inner SELF is not seen. The respect for "one's self" brings the abundant life. Do Jesus and Paul agree as to the value of a person?
Meditation: May our neighbor sense our inner spirit! May the love of God in me keep me humble. May I never become presumptuous! *Amen.*

December 10
LOVE KNITS TOGETHER

"That their hearts may be encouraged as they are knit together in love." (Colossians 2:2a)

The letter to the Colossians argues for the New Covenant of the Spirit in exchange for the old legalistic ways. Love in action should knit people together as into a finished fabric.

Love becomes the bond of perfectness that produces a heart of compassion, kindness, lowliness, meekness, forbearance, long suffering and forgiveness which tend to activate others in love. An understanding of love involves the acceptance of that which is each man's own personal possession. Do you use yourself to build or to destroy? Are you well acquainted with your real SELF?

Meditation: We know that of our own volition the bond of love unites us with You. May I know You so well that my conscience may be alert to scold me when I am wrong and praise me when I do right! *Amen.*

December 11
ROOTED AND GROUNDED IN LOVE

"Being rooted and grounded in love may have power to comprehend . . . what is the breadth and length, and height, and depth, and to know the love of Christ which surpasses knowledge, that you may be filled with all the fullness of God."
(Ephesians 3:17-19)

This is another effort to define the scope of love. Notice its comprehensiveness. The practice of love is shown in Paul's letter to Philemon, when he asked Philemon to receive Onesimus as a fellow human being now that he had become a Christian. Love is presented as a norm of action within the inner selves, in that all three, Paul, Philemon and Onesimus, were rooted and grounded in love. All could comprehend the love of God through Christ and, therefore, knew that to practice love was to be in the fullness of God. Is it true that when one is revengeful he makes for himself a divided SELF? To keep the SELF together and knit it with other selves is love at work.

Meditation: May the mercy of God, like the grace and favor of God, be received each day so that the love with which Jesus loved may be real. *Amen.*

December 12
THE MIND OF LOVE

"Complete my joy by being of the same mind, having the same love." (Philippians 2:2)

The letters of Paul to the various church people emphasize love as the medium of judgment, decision and action through which the New Covenant was to be made effective and efficient. Love should coordinate the minds of people so that "whatever is pure, honorable, just, lovely, of good report would be emphasized and the minds and opinions of the people would have a constructive and positive content." (cf. Philippians 4:8f)

Meditation: "Love divine, all love excelling, Joy of heav'n to
        earth come down.

        Jesus, thou art all compassion, Pure, unbounded
        love thou art."

                              lines from hymn by Charles Wesley

December 13
THE ULTIMATE CHARGE

"The aim of our charge is love that issues from a pure heart and a good conscience and sincere faith." (1 Timothy 1:5)

This first letter to Timothy aims to encourage the young man to preach and to practice the positive message of love. The complete SELF or PERSON must be committed to God in love. The idea of Christ as a ransom and redeemer should make one become an example in word, manner of life, love, faith and purity. There is no higher principle for Christian action than that of love and it is interesting that the canon of the New Testament contains books that consistently agree on love as the medium of Christian fellowship.

Meditation: May the advice to Timothy be regarded as good advice to people of this generation. May the mastery of the

SELF make me efficient in teaching the power of love with faith in Christ! *Amen.*

December 14
FAITH AND LOVE AS A PATTERN

"Follow the pattern of the sound words which you have heard from me, in the faith and love which are in Christ Jesus." (2 Timothy 1:14)

Paul could now use himself as a pattern. Sound words may be those that have stood the test of time and do not have to be untaught because they have universal content and sound philosophy. The basic principle of his words were faith, hope and love in Christ. A man had many places in his Bible marked with the letters T and P. When he was asked what they meant he said Tried and Proved. Can we say that Paul and other New Testament authors had tried and proved the love of Christ as a basis of action and the medium through which the New Covenant may be fulfilled?

Meditation: "Not with the hope of gaining aught;
        Not seeking a reward,
        But as thyself hast loved me
        O ever loving Lord."

                stanza from hymn by Edward Caswall

December 15
THE ROYAL LAW OF LOVE

"If you really fulfill the royal law according to the scripture, you shall love your neighbor as yourself." (James 2:8)

James does not like discrimination. With faith one becomes a doer of the law of love and not a hearer only. The Royal Law embodies neighborliness with the SELF projecting itself in acts of love. The SELF or PERSON is the medium through which we have fellowship with another. Does love grounded in God help the SELF to project and radiate love? James, in searching for the highest term to describe the love of a neighbor as oneself, used the word "royal law." Can you think of a better name? We should be careful about personalizing things lest we weaken our notion of God's love. We like flowers but we love God. We like dogs but we love our neighbors with the same love and respect that we have for ourselves. As persons we can think only of God as a person. A dog is not a person.

Meditation: "Not for myself alone may my prayer be,
       But lift Your world, O Christ, through me."
       Amen.

December 16
FERVENT IN LOVE

"Above all hold unfailing your love for one another." (1 Peter 4:8a)

This letter must have strengthened the faith of the early Christians as they faced persecutions. They needed to be bound together in their love one with another. To do this they knitted themselves together with the love of God Who first loved them. This appreciation of God's love supported their prayers and knitted the strength of the brotherhood against ignorant and bigoted persecutors. When we love God supremely the love for our neighbor becomes more genuine and supreme. Do you think that loving your neighbor as yourself has a tendency to weaken your love of God?

Meditation: "May the grace of Christ our Saviour, and the
       Father's boundless Love
       With the Holy Spirit's favor,
       Rest upon us from above."

                    stanza from hymn "From the
                         table now retiring"
                         Author: John Rowe

December 17

LOVE COVERS SINS

"Love covers a multitude of sins." (1 Peter 4:8b) (cf. James 5:20) (Proverbs 10:12)

It is better to suffer for doing well than for wrongdoing. We sin but we can repent. Peter had this experience. When we ask God to forgive then we should be willing to devote ourselves to God and His kingdom by thinking and doing the will of God. In that way we may think that our sins are being covered with good deeds. In a sense our sins become canceled through righteousness. The love of God has taken the place of the love of the world and good deeds and a harmonious spirit follows. Do people tend to be more forgiving if they cancel a former wrong by a present right? Do you think we should be afraid to do wrong because the love of God and His grace is so magnanimous? Do some people sin, ask forgiveness and then continue to do wrong? Can we cultivate right habits easier than wrong habits?

Meditation: We are told that if we suffer for righteousness sake we are blessed. May we, therefore, give our blessing, and offer our prayers for those who revile us and reject our good will! *Amen.*

December 18

FAITH IN THE NEW COVENANT

"Let us consider how to stir up one another to love and good works." (Hebrews 10:24)

The book of the Hebrews, like other books of the New Testament, exalts love as a Christian value to effect the New Covenant. The laws of God are in the heart and written upon the mind. God exists and those who choose to respond to Him are His people. Birth, age, time or place have nothing to do about determining who are the people of God. It is what each SELF or person does with himself or herself that counts. To

24

LOVE CASTS OUT FEAR

ve casts out fear." (1 John 4:18b)

ne has love there need be no fear. We do not fear
parents. You may be certain that God is as
f us and our way of life as our parents. It is well-
t sin creates fear. If fear exists in us, then we need
d to be counseled to get rid of the cause of fear
e area within our being where love should work.
ar we should have is that of doing wrong because
transgression of the SELF and the Royal Law of
ed not fear God because God forgives and receives
n we are sinners. He always loves us and we can-
Him.

May the love of God make me fear to transgress
ve. May the vicarious love of my parents, rela-
nds help me to be strong in spirit and in truth!

D'S LOVE IS IMMEASURABLE

*loved the world that he gave his only Son, that
es in Him should not perish but have eternal
:16)*

al day of Jesus we are aware that God loved
gave Himself through His Son so that we may
depth, height, breadth and width of His love.
measure God is as futile as to measure love,
imit to God and His love. There was no meas-
t in the angel's song "Glory to God in the
earth peace among men with whom he is well
2:14)

y Christ be born again in me today. May my
him and his service bring joy to the angels.

---

choose to serve God is the highest choice and makes that
SELF a chosen person of God. God is Spirit. He is Love.
Christians are urged by the author to encourage one another
to love in spirit and in truth and to do good. Persecution is
to be expected but God and His love is greater than anything
that the enemies of the grace of God may do.
Meditation: Help us now and always to endure temptation
by overcoming evil with good. Let us be in the world but not
of the evils of the world! *Amen.*

December 19

LOVE IS WORLD WIDE

*"Let brotherly love continue. Do not neglect to show hos-
pitality to strangers."* (Hebrews 13:1-2)

This philosophical book exalts the New Covenant and
with it the idea of the priesthood of all believers. As the fathers
and prophets were sustained by faith and their works are
known through the Bible as history, so the Christians are
urged to have faith and to cultivate love among themselves.
This love would manifest itself in Christian fellowship with no
limits or boundaries.
Meditation: May good will and brotherly love continue to
prevail in our neighborhoods, our churches and our nations.
Where there is evil, bring good; where there is doubt, bring
faith; where there is unhappiness, bring joy through Christ,
our Redeemer! *Amen.*

December 20

THE MERCY OF GOD IS FORTHCOMING

*"Keep yourselves in the love of God, wait for the mercy of
our Lord Jesus Christ unto eternal life."* (Jude 1:21)

Wise persons will commit themselves to Christ as their
Saviour. Jude warns them of the judgment of God. If their
lives are filled with love, God will receive them without blem-

ish. The enemies of Christ become frustrated and will do evil to Christians without any limit. God, however, is in control and if one keeps himself in the love of God he cannot ultimately fail. Love is based on devotion more than emotion. It is based on intelligence which leads to devotion. Do some people substitute emotion and desire for love?

Meditation: It requires effort to keep oneself in the love of God. Mercy, however, is available and if we sustain our love the mercy of God will avail. May our interests, associations, etc., be kept on an intellectual level! *Amen.*

December 21
LOVE LOOSES US FROM SINS

"To Him who loves us and has freed us from our sins by His blood and made us a kingdom, priests to his God and Father." (Revelation 1:5c-6a)

The book of Revelation aims to strengthen the persecuted. Having the love of God to support them and being made free through forgiveness from sin, paradise will be attained. (Revelation 3:21) The description of Paradise is visionary but it is clear that it is a condition where unrighteousness shall not be. It is a condition of the Spirit wherein love reigns supremely. Is it now the task of man to get back into Paradise from which, because of sin, he allowed himself to be driven?

Meditation: It is a spiritual joy and privilege to be loosed from sin and to be in a country where one is free to worship. *Amen.*

December 22
GOD IS LOVE

"God is love, and he who abides in love abides in God and God abides in him." (1 John 4:16)

Step by step we have gone and have finally reached the

point where we have the aut
love, marital love, filial love
have persisted and each in t
central theme of love, so th
qualification GOD IS LOVE.
being a Loving Spirit give
abide in Him so that there
are bound together with
points upward and holds
upward and holds our ar
outward so love spreads
mankind.

Meditation: We are ha
and that we may love
and ours encircle all
produced by the rain

December 23

"We love, because h

Being created in
something of Hims
handiwork. The di
in us. No wonder
is not pleasing to
duty and privileg
men. Having firs
tinually confront
ship. If God lov
we love God's
Meditation: W
If our parents
are at one wi
make a day o

Decembe

"Perfect
When
our lovin
solicitous
known tha
to pray a
and find t
The only f
wrong is th
God. We ne
us even whe
not escape
Meditation:
the law of
tions and fri
Amen.

December 25
GO
"For God so
whoever belie
life." (John 3
On this nat
all people and
experience the
To attempt to
for there is no
ure or limit se
highest, and on
pleased." (Luke
Meditation: Ma
commitment to

May the messages of the angels, the worship of the shepherds and the gifts of the wise men quicken us anew with His love! *Amen.*

December 26
THE LOVE OF CHILDREN STEMS FROM GOD

"By this we know that we love the children of God, when we love God and obey his commandments." (1 John 5:2)

John believed that from the beginning we were taught to love one another. Cain showed his lack of love when he killed Abel. But the grace of God preserved Cain although his deed was evil. He became a fugitive. Sin makes fugitives and prodigals. Love makes a home. (1 John 3:10c) It is interesting how repeatedly the New Testament books state that obedience to the commandments stem from love and is a criterion of the depth of our love to God. This space age is teaching us again how closely we are bound together. May this space age pinpoint the fact that since we are bound together we are going to stay together in love. Is the love of God essential to implement peace among the nations? What shall we do about the unbelievers, the disbelievers, the unloved and those who do not choose to love?

Meditation: May the love of God be a certainty with me! May the fact of God's love for me strengthen my faith in the fact that all who choose to be children of God are sons of God. *Amen.*

December 27
WE ARE GOD'S CHILDREN

"See what love the Father has given us, that we should be called children of God." (1 John 3:1)

To be a child of the Creator of the universe is a great favor of grace. It places us beyond the animal level and even the constellations in space. We are free to choose, and to have faith, hope and love. Jesus, the Son of God, as a brother assumed and accepted God from the beginning. His parents accepted Jesus coming from God. Some of his kindred brothers joined with the early Christians and accepted Him as the Son of God, the Messiah, the anointed of God. Should we appreciate the high honor that God has given to us, to be called children of God?

Meditation: We worship, we honor, we adore, we love You, O God. *Amen.*

December 28
THE PURITY OF GOD PURIFIES US

"We shall see him even as he is. And everyone who thus hopes in him purifies himself as he is pure." (1 John 3:2c-4)

The question of being made pure must have risen among the early Christians and John concluded that the hope of seeing God inspires us to cleanse ourselves from sin and to keep ourselves unspotted from a world where sin is made alluring. With God and heaven there is nothing unclean. Deception, suspicion or anything evil do not abide in God's kingdom. To edify the SELF is not selfish but is a duty and privilege. The SELF is your personality at work. We may be creatures of the dust but we are also privileged to be accounted as children of God. Dwight L. Moody was among the first Americans to preach and proclaim consistently that God was love and it led him into the abundant life. We may say that it also made him eternal as God is eternal. Do you know the tremendous outreach of Dwight L. Moody?

Meditation: O God, our heart becomes a heart of love when we love You. Your purity helps us to be pure. Your will makes our wills to be ONE will! *Amen.*

December 29

WALK IN LOVE

"And this is love, that we follow his commandments; this is the commandment you have heard from the beginning, that you follow love." (2 John 6)
"Follow after love." (1 Corinthians 14:1)

It is only natural that since God is Love we should live according to the teachings that have been given to us through the commandments, inspiration and revelation. The commandments and requirements of Christian living are not grievous but in keeping with the imagination of the best SELF. When we live and work with God our consciences become clear and we delight to worship Him.

Meditation: May Your love become my love and may we never be separated. May I be raised to be eternally with You and all who worship You. *Amen.*

December 30

DOING GOOD IS OF GOD

"He who does good is of God." (3 John 11)
"Every one who believes that Jesus is the Christ is a child of God and everyone who loves the parent loves the child." (1 John 5:1)

Belief is a confirmation of opinion or judgment. When we accept or assume God as our Heavenly Father, our beliefs confirm our relation to Him. Worship and Christian service naturally follows. We do what we believe is worth doing. Since God is the Supreme Power we try to make the personality or SELF be at ONE with God. As we grow in knowledge and grace, God's Spirit confirms our discipleship and God's love becomes at one with ours. This makes a parent and child relationship. Does the love of God abide in you?

Meditation: Help us to cover unrighteousness with deeds of

righteousness and it may be that in time unrighteousness will
be overcome with righteousness and spiritual peace will prevail. *Amen.*

December 31
CHILDREN LOVE ONE ANOTHER

"God abides in us and his love is perfected in us." (1 John
4:12c)

God is perfect. (Matthew 5:48) As we seek to better our
condition and relationship with God we may expect improve-
ment. There is a tradition that John, the beloved disciple,
lived to be very old. When he became feeble his friends
carried or wheeled him from one place to another. As children came close to his carriage he would say "little children love one another." He gave what he had received. By
uniting the love of God with his own love, he loved others
and manifested the trinity of love which is the Love of God
to us, our love of God and our love toward one another.

Meditation: "For the love of God is broader,
            Than the measure of man's mind;
            And the heart of the Eternal
            Is most wonderfully kind."

                                        stanza from Hymn by
                                        Frederick W. Faber

INDEX